International
Economic Policy

International Economic Policy

Beyond the Trade and Debt Crisis

John Charles Pool
Charles Pool & Associates

Stephen C. Stamos, Jr.
Bucknell University

Lexington Books
D.C. Heath and Company/Lexington, Massachusetts/Toronto

The authors and publisher express their thanks to those who have granted permission to reproduce copyrighted text. The copyright acknowledgments appear on page 144.

Library of Congress Cataloging-in-Publication Data

Pool, John Charles.
    International economic policy.

    Bibliography: p.
    Includes index.
    1. International economic relations. I. Stamos, Stephen C. II Title.
HF1359.P66   1989   337   88-7912
ISBN 0-669-17109-3
ISBN 0-669-17110-7 (pbk.)

Published simultaneously in Canada
Printed in the United States of America
Casebound International Standard Book Number: 0-669-17109-3
Paperbound International Standard Book Number: 0-669-17110-7
Library of Congress Catalog Card Number: 88-7912

The paper used in this publication meets the minimum requirements of American National Standard for Information Sciences—Permanence of Paper for Printed Library Materials, ANSI Z39.48-1984. ∞™

90 91 92 8 7 6 5 4 3

Contents

Figures

Tables

Preface and Acknowledgments

The later years of the 1980s have been at once perplexing and paradoxical for economists and others brave enough to call themselves analysts of economic trends. In some ways, those years were good times. By 1988 the U.S. economy had entered its sixth year of continuous economic expansion—the longest peacetime period of steady growth since World War II. By most measures things were going very well indeed. Unemployment hovered at low rates, as did inflation, while the economy operated at near-record levels of capacity utilization.

But there was a growing sense of uneasiness—heightened by the historic stock market crash—that the underlying trends were not as rosy as the apparent superficial prosperity. The national debt more than doubled under a frugal administration, corporate debt exploded in the wake of an unprecedented merger takeover movement, the United States became a net foreign debtor nation, and the Third World debt burden threatened the integrity of the international financial system. And there was a growing consensus that these trends could not be sustained.

Many recognized the problem, and some proposed solutions, but nothing was done. The 1988 U.S. election campaign, which some thought would clarify the issues, only served to obscure them. Not one solid long-run proposal came out of the campaign.

In this book we hope to rectify that problem somewhat by examining the issues in both historical and current context and, especially, by analyzing the myriad of proposed solutions in an orderly and, we hope, understandable fashion that will be accessible to both the lay reader and college students, who have the largest stake in it all.

We think these problems could be resolved if there were enlightened leadership that understood the necessity of coordinated worldwide economic policy and the need for all players to sacrifice the short-run illusion of prosperity to the longer-run goal of stability. But, chances are that will not happen until the external forces that are now destabilizing the world economy impose a solution on us that will be very painful for everyone.

We owe a great debt to the many writers who have had the courage and prescience to point out that the emperor has no clothes. Among them are Michael Blumenthal, Irving Friedman, Harry Magdoff, Alfred Malabre, Morris Miller, Michael Moffit, Peter Peterson, Robert Reich, Felix Rohatyn, Alan Sinai, and Paul Sweezy. And there are many more.

Among those who contributed more directly to this particular project are Professors James Crotty of the University of Massachusetts–Amherst, Ross M. LaRoe of Denison University, and Tom Riddell of Smith College, who reviewed the manuscript in its earlier stages and who agreed with at least some of our analysis.

In this computerized world it is hard to remember what it was like to write a book without word processors, computer generated graphics, and that wonderful invention, the spell-check. But, that aside, Linda Vollmer processed the words with a diligence and patience far beyond what anyone could reasonably expect. The art and statistical presentations were prepared by Stacy Michel, who has a unique capacity to translate our hieroglyphics into an easily understandable form, which we think exceeds that of any of our previous books.

Last, but hardly least, we have to acknowledge our debt to our families: Betty, Mike, and Laura Linda; Lucy, Barry, and Lisanna, who continue to have faith that what we do is worthwhile and that—sometime—one of our books will make enough money to allow us to do our fair share in reducing the federal budget deficit.

Introduction

It is well known, if not universally recognized, that the international economy has reached a level of imbalance that approaches crisis proportions. The steady erosion of the once-dominant position of the United States in the world economic arena, coupled with the rapid rise of Japan, West Germany, and the so-called newly industrialized countries (NICs) of the Pacific rim to a position of unparalleled economic power, means that the international economic system will be drastically reordered in the coming decade, if not sooner. The problems can be ignored, but they will not go away. Adjustments will have to be made. The pressing question facing policymakers and monetary authorities is whether the adjustments will be planned and orderly or chaotic.

The problem revolves around three major developments, all of which were unexpected, and none is sustainable. Each development is a story in itself, but each is interrelated. The first, and probably least understood, development is the staggering Third World foreign debt, which dates back to the early 1970s. That debt, which now exceeds $1 trillion, is threatening the stability of the international financial system as it compounds to astronomical levels. Many solutions have been proposed, but none has been implemented in a way that alleviates the problem. As a consequence of mounting debt servicing obligations, standards of living in the underdeveloped world have been pushed back to levels lower than they were twenty-five years ago.

The second development, which is better understood but just as serious, is the unprecedented recent explosion of the U.S. federal budget and balance-of-payments deficit—the twin deficits, as they are called. As a consequence of record-high federal deficits beginning in 1981, the U.S. national debt more than doubled in only five years. Interest payments on this debt are the third largest category in the federal budget—after defense and social security—and are causing a massive transfer of wealth from the tax-paying middle class to the bond-owning upper class. If the debt were internally owned, it would still be a problem but not an unsustainable trend. Increasingly, however, the debt is being purchased by foreign interests that are awash in dollars accumulated from the trade imbalance. The result is that the United States has been pushed into a net foreign debtor position for the first time since 1914.

This third development, the U.S. foreign debt, which exceeded $400 billion at the end of 1987, represents the excess of foreign-held assets in the United States over the total of foreign assets held by U.S. citizens and corporations. For most of the post–World War II period the buildup of U.S. assets abroad, which was mostly due to the globalization of the production process spearheaded by U.S.-based multinational corporations, meant that the United States could count on a net surplus of foreign investment income in its current account to offset negative trade balances. This changed dramatically in 1985 as the ever-growing trade deficits overwhelmed declining net investment income, reversing the once-dominant position of the United States in the international economy.

At the same time that the United States was becoming the world's largest debtor nation, Japan became the world's largest creditor, followed closely by West Germany. A creditor nation has two options: it can invest the funds earned from its export surplus into its own development and toward raising its own standard of living, or it can invest the funds in the country with which it has a trade imbalance. Largely Japan has chosen to recycle its export surpluses back to the United States by purchasing U.S. Treasury bonds, corporate stock, and to a lesser—but rapidly increasing—extent by directly investing in U.S. plant and equipment or real estate. Thus a mutually dependent relationship between the two nations has evolved over a very short time span.

Japanese investments have supplemented the now-feeble U.S. savings rate and served to finance U.S. federal budget deficits, thereby allowing American consumers to maintain the high standards of living they have become accustomed to. This has meant that the U.S. economy has become almost completely dependent on the infusion of Japanese capital funds that could be withdrawn at will, pushing the financial markets into chaos, if not collapse, and the United States into a severe recession that would reverberate throughout the world. This has meant that the traditional tools of monetary and fiscal policy have become obsolete. The United States has lost control of its own economic destiny.

Japan and the other trade surplus–creditor countries have little option but to recycle their surpluses back to the United States. The U.S. addiction to Japanese imports has provided the engine of growth for Japan. Without U.S. markets, which are far and away their largest, the Japanese would be forced to look elsewhere for outlets for levels of production that far exceed their own traditional consumption patterns. Since there are no comparable markets, the relationship has become almost totally symbiotic. But in the process it is Japan, not the United States, that holds the upper hand. The trend toward larger and larger amounts of Japanese direct, as opposed to portfolio, investments in the United States reinforce the mutual interdependence patterns. A Honda plant in Ohio or a downtown office building in Los Angeles cannot be disposed of overnight as U.S. Treasury bonds can. Soon, if it does not already, Japan and other foreign investors will have almost as big a stake in the U.S. economy as does the United States itself.

Traditional theories of international trade and finance, which have been around since the early eighteenth century, suggest that this uncomfortable situation could be adjusted into some semblance of balance either automatically, through free market exchange rate movements, or in a planned manner through intervention in the foreign exchange markets. Both have been tried; neither has worked. The strong dollar of the early 1980s, which was a result of increased demand for dollars as the surplus countries sought to reap the benefits of artificially high interest rates in the United States, exacerbated the trade imbalance to crisis proportions. The coordinated intervention that began in the fall of 1985—and resulted in a 50 percent depreciation in the value of the dollar against the currencies of the major U.S. trading partners—did little to ameliorate the situation. By 1988 the U.S. trade and current account balances were still at record highs.

It has become clear that something must be done to reorder the international economy toward a cooperative system that accounts for the rapid role reversal we have witnessed over the past few years. It is not realistic to continue acting as if the United States, and particularly the U.S. dollar, can continue to play the key dominant role in the world economy that it has for the past forty years. No nation can act as police force of the world, the buyer of last resort, the creditor of last resort, and the keeper of the key currency while at the same time becoming the world's largest debtor. The arithmetic does not add up. Rethinking that reality is the theme of this book. There are, we shall argue, ways in which the system can be brought back into balance without undue harm to the key players and, especially, to the innocent but interested bystanders in the Third World, who have already paid their dues but received nothing in return. They, more than anyone, hold the power to bring down the house of cards.

In chapter 1 we trace the history of these unprecedented developments from the demise of the gold standard and the dollar-based Bretton Woods system to the oil price shock of the 1970s and the concomitant development of the Third World debt crisis. Efforts to ameliorate the increasing trade imbalances through exchange rate manipulation are then analyzed, with some emphasis on the role of the U.S. dollar as a faltering key currency.

In chapter 2, the buildup of the triple debt crisis—the U.S. internal and external debts and the Third World debt—is analyzed in historical and current context, again with some emphasis on the role of the United States.

The question of why the current international financial system is not up to the task of bringing the system back into balance is taken up in chapter 3, which analyzes in some detail the myriad of schemes that have been proposed to correct the situation. We argue that none of the proposals is adequate unless they are taken in the broader context of a new system of international economic policy coordination. For such a system to be implemented, an international conference on the order of Bretton Woods will be necessary, this time with Japan, West Germany, the NICs and, especially, the Third World debtor countries at the table.

No fundamental changes can take place without the cooperation and, indeed, insistence of the largest player in the game, the United States, which still has an economy more than twice as large as Japan and West Germany put together. Chapter 4 therefore takes up the question of how the United States could creatively face up to its dilemma and take the lead in instituting changes before it is forced to.

Then chapter 5 focuses on the rapid changes taking place in the other industrialized countries, with emphasis on Japan and West Germany, and tried to explain why neither seems willing or able to take the mantle of world economic leadership.

Finally, in chapter 6, we consider the various policy options that must be implemented if this increasingly serious situation is to be resolved.

1

The International Financial System
in Historical Perspective

A delicate but decisive transition is under way. It is a transition from stop-go policies and inflationary expansion to a program of monetary and fiscal stability aimed at sustained growth. A good start has been made. But persistence and international cooperation are now required to insure that the needed growth occurs, while further progress is made in removing imbalances. . . .

For their part, the developing countries can best improve their growth performance and their access to credit markets by their choice of macro-economic and structural policies.

Significant progress has been made over the past few years. Economic policies are now better attuned to economic realities, and inflation—which had been poisoning the financial system for fifteen years—has finally been brought under control in the industrial world.

But much remains to be done. External payments imbalances among the larger industrial countries are a disturbing source of instability and tensions. The erosion of commodity prices has adversely affected the developing countries at the very time when they more than ever need increased export earnings to grow and to service their debts.

In a world that is increasingly interdependent, it is proving more complex than ever to cope with these problems. A satisfactory solution requires not only an understanding of the interaction among national economic policies but also firm adherence to the fundamental principles of monetary stability and strengthened commitment to international cooperation.

Economic policy coordination among industrial countries is no longer a matter of theoretical preference. It is instead a prerequisite for growth with stability. Industrial countries must work together to complete the process of disinflation, to maximize the sources of economic growth, and to assure an open international trading system.

—Jacques de Larosiere, former managing director,
International Monetary Fund[1]

International finance is a complex web of exchange rates, international agreements (and disagreements), balance of payments, letters of credit, hedging, arbitrage, current accounts, capital accounts, and, most important for our purposes here, credit arrangements between nations. It is a system highly dependent on political nuances, power politics, and economic policies.

But in many ways it is merely a system of gentlemen's agreements to which all nations abide so that international trade, with all of its presumed benefits, can take place. When it functions smoothly and equitably, everyone benefits. When it does not, everyone loses. Over the past few decades, the web of international finance has become so tangled that the losers far outnumber the winners. The system is slowly collapsing under its own weight. To understand why, one must understand the history of the problem.

The Enigmatic Role of Gold

It is commonly thought that gold historically has played a major role in international trade transactions. Because gold is scarce and virtually indestructible, it has been used as a standard of monetary exchange since antiquity. Wars have been fought over it, nations conquered and exploited for it. Indeed, for centuries, many nations based their international economic policies on the—now curious—assumption that the accumulation of gold brought with it wealth and well-being. This belief, which we now refer to as mercantilism, dominated economic thinking from 1500 to 1750 and inspired Adam Smith to write *The Wealth of Nations,* which laid the groundwork for modern theories of international trade and caused many of the problems the world now faces.

Paradoxically the times during which the world was on the international gold standard are still referred to as the "good old days of the gold standard." They were not, in fact, such good times, and they did not last very long. The gold standard, which is but one of several ways to arrange international economic affairs, existed in its pure variation for only about forty years, roughly from 1875 to 1914. Gold functions well as a standard of monetary value and exchange only so long as every nation agrees to value its currency equal to a given weight of gold and so long as gold is freely tradable internationally. International disruptions, most notably wars, tend to bring out everyone's regard for their own interests, and under such conditions international agreements tend to fall by the wayside. This was the fate of the gold standard during World War I when it was abandoned, much to the chagrin of those disposed to nostalgia.

Beyond the difficulties of ignoring self-interest under duress, gold exchange standard agreements are a cumbersome and inconvenient way to handle international financial transactions. This is partly because it is expensive, if not ridiculous, to ship gold between countries to settle balance-of-payments disequilibria but more important because the gold standard extracts a high degree of economic discipline domestically as well as internationally. This is inconvenient for the stronger players in the game of international trade and can be disastrous for the minor leaguers.

A gold standard requires that nations maintain a favorable (or equilibrium) balance of trade and payments or come up with the difference in gold. That means that countries with trade deficits lose their gold supply to those with trade surpluses and/or that they institute appropriate economic policies to correct the (perceived) undesirable situation. That is, they must put in place deflationary domestic policies (to increase unemployment and slow down economic growth) to decrease the price of their exports, which will allow them to become more competitive internationally. At the same time often-needed imports are reduced because of the lower overall domestic demand.

Such discipline can be politically inconvenient in certain situations. Accordingly the gold standard was abandoned by most of the major economic powers during the early years of the Great Depression. Although there were numerous attempts to revive it during the 1930s, gold did not resurface as a monetary standard until after World War II, when it was linked in a tenuous fashion to the U.S. dollar, which replaced gold as the international medium of exchange. This development was to have far-reaching consequences.

The Bretton Woods Conference

The United States emerged from World War II not only as a military victor but as an economic victor as well. It was by far the strongest economic power in the world. By 1945 it had accumulated some $25 billion in gold reserves, almost 75 percent of the world's gold supply.

The United States was in a powerful position to reorganize the international financial system to serve its own best interests. Gold, almost everyone agreed, was clearly not up to the task of providing the necessary liquidity to finance world trade. The price of gold had been set at $35 an ounce by President Roosevelt in 1933, but the general price level had almost doubled since then, so gold was an underpriced commodity, scarce even for commercial uses. Clearly a new system was needed.

With the war winding down and victory apparent, the monetary authorities of the leading Allied nations gathered at Bretton Woods, New Hampshire, in 1944 to work out a new international monetary arrangement. The delegation from Great Britain, headed by economist John Maynard Keynes, argued that an international central bank should be established to monitor trade imbalances and with the power to force deficit countries to adjust their economic policies any time deficits drifted out of line. But turning the power of control over domestic economic policy to an international institution was more than most countries could accept, and the United States, in essence, vetoed any such plan.

Out of that meeting came one of the more dramatic historical examples of what is sometimes referred to as the Golden Rule: "Whoever has the gold makes the rules." The gold standard was replaced with the dollar standard, and the United States was accordingly exempted from the traditional discipline of international finance. The United States, since it had most of the world's gold supply, agreed to make the dollar "as good as gold," redeemable on demand by any central bank at the rate of $35 an ounce. This meant the dollar became the accepted medium of exchange for international transactions. This seemingly routine development was to have far-reaching implications for the international financial system, certainly far beyond what anyone would have imagined at the time.

Since the dollar was now as good as gold, the rest of the world could, and did, use dollars instead of gold to settle international payments, for international transactions in general, and for their own reserves. The system was generally acceptable to most of the Bretton Woods participants (with the notable exception of France). Dollars were more liquid than gold and did not have to be stored or shipped. Most important, dollar deposits can earn interest (gold, in contrast, gathers dust in a bank vault).

The new system did not exempt anyone (except the United States, which could create money and spend it at will) from the discipline of international finance. Now dollars, instead of gold, provided that discipline. All national currencies were now tied to the dollar instead of gold. The dollar, in turn, was pegged to gold at the rate of $35 an ounce. Trade imbalances now had to be settled in U.S. dollars. The Bretton Woods Conference had made the dollar the world's key currency, and in so doing the stage was set for an unprecedented series of developments.

The Bretton Woods Conference also established a quasi-international bank: the International Monetary Fund (IMF). The IMF was created to monitor and discipline trade and to provide temporary loans to countries with balance-of-payments problems. Such loans were conditioned on deficit countries' "getting their house in order" promptly: slowing down their inflation rate and stimulating their export sector and/or reducing imports, if they were running trade deficits. Funds for the IMF operation were provided by contributions from member nations, which in turn had a vote in its operations proportional to their contribution. The United States, which made the largest contribution, had the controlling vote. It was no coincidence that the headquarters of the IMF was located in Washington, D.C.

Evolution of the Dollar Glut

The new system worked well for a number of years. So long as the United States held a large percentage of the world's gold supply, other countries were willing to accept dollars in payment for international transactions. Under such conditions the United States could run trade deficits at will and simply pay for the difference with dollars. But in the early years of the agreement, this did not happen because the United States was consistently running trade surpluses, which, in fact, caused a dollar shortage, something hard to imagine now (figure 1–1). Since then the world has moved from a dollar shortage to a dollar glut. How and why this happened is crucial to understanding the current international situation.

First, we must remember that, by definition, balance-of-payments accounts must always be in balance. To put it another way, total dollar expenditures abroad by the United States must equal total dollar receipts for the rest of the world. This means that if the United States is running an export surplus—exporting more than it is importing—it must provide the means to finance it, through loans, gifts, or foreign investments. There is no other way for a country to get the dollars needed to purchase U.S. goods.

In the years just following World War II, the United States was running huge export surpluses and was at the same time providing the wherewithal

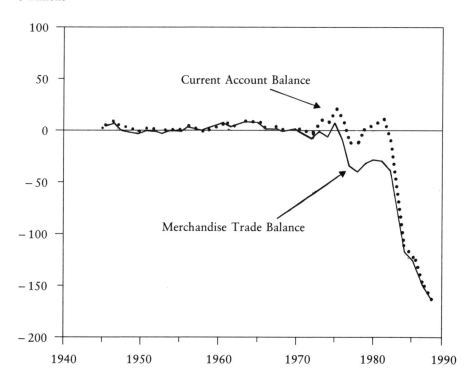

Source: U.S. Department of Commerce, *Survey of Current Business*, Vol. 68, No. 6, June 1988.

Figure 1–1. U.S. Current Account and Trade Balance, 1946–1987

to pay for them. The United States ran a huge balance-of-trade surplus—almost $32 billion—during the 1946–1949 postwar period as it furnished much-needed capital goods to the war-damaged countries of Europe. But since by definition, balance-of-payments accounts must always balance, something else had to happen in the other accounts to offset this large credit item. In this case, the credits in the current account were largely balanced by debits in the capital account in the form of loans and grants made to the European countries under the Marshall Plan. If these loans had not been made, it would have been impossible for the United States to run such large trade surpluses. During this early period this caused no special problem with the international monetary system since the United States was easily able to make these loans. In fact, if anything, it had a positive effect on the U.S. economy and the rest of the world.

But soon all that began to change. Between 1950 and 1957, the United States not only financed its exports surplus but overfinanced it, so that the rest of the world began to accumulate dollar balances to the tune of almost $9 billion by the end of that seven-year period. At the same time, the United States began to lose some gold as part of these dollar balances were cashed in. This was a clear indicator of trouble but was not considered by most economists to be a serious problem at the time.

The situation began to change rapidly around 1958. Between 1958 and 1965 the United States still maintained a balance-of-trade surplus and continued granting loans and foreign aid and increasing its investments abroad. But the total value of these loans and grants far exceeded the U.S. trade surplus, and large dollar balances began to be accumulated by the rest of the world. This was the beginning of the so-called dollar glut, which is still with us and remains a significant factor in the current international financial crisis.

The Eurodollar Market

By the early 1960s another significant event occurred, this one also with far-reaching implications: the development of the so-called Eurodollar market. Eurodollars are dollars deposited in any bank (not necessarily in Europe) outside the United States and kept there as dollar-denominated deposits. European banks, many of them heavily involved in foreign trade transactions, found it convenient to begin accepting dollar deposits and using them in their day-to-day business. This avoided bothersome exchange transactions and earned them interest as well. And since the dollar was backed by gold, this development seemed not only logical but safe to everyone concerned.

There was one serious catch, however. U.S. banks are required to maintain a percentage of their deposits as reserves. This requirement limits the extent to which they can expand their asset base by loaning out deposits since they must keep a portion of them as reserves. By controlling this reserve requirement, the U.S. Federal Reserve Bank (the U.S. central bank) can maintain some control over the U.S. money supply. An increase in the reserve requirement, for example, causes a contraction of the money supply and is a powerful, but not often used, monetary policy tool. But foreign banks in general have no such requirement. As a result Eurodollar deposits could be expanded infinitely through a process called the multiple expansion of deposits; since there are no reserve requirements, there are no limits to banks' ability to create money.

In addition, European banks are allowed to pay interest on very short-term deposits, while U.S. banking laws require that a deposit must be held for at least thirty days before any interest can be paid. Since the 1960s was a period of rapid expansion of U.S. multinational corporate (MNC) activities around the world, many MNCs, which routinely move large sums of surplus funds between countries to finance their offshore production activities, found Eurodollar deposits to be an attractive option compared to holding their surpluses in U.S. banks. Accordingly large sums moved into the Eurodollar market.

The result was the creation of an entirely new money supply, based on and denominated in dollars. There were two effects. One was that the U.S. bank authorities lost control of a large portion of the U.S. money supply, which severely reduced their ability to control inflation with monetary policy, one of the primary macroeconomic policy tools. The other was that it solidified the role of the U.S. dollar as the cornerstone of the international monetary system. Now Eurodollar deposits amount to more than $2 trillion (the exact amount is unknown), which is roughly equal to the basic U.S. money supply itself. Half of the U.S. dollars in existence are outside any kind of control whatsoever by the U.S. banking authorities, which, among other things, makes it easier to understand why the entire world maintains a lively interest in the health of the U.S. economy and, especially, the U.S. rate of inflation.

The Demise of Gold

The other relevant (and unexpected) development that occurred in the 1960s was that the United States continued to run balance-of-trade deficits, and its gold supply began to dwindle. Although in theory anyone should have been willing to accept dollars in payment for international trade transactions (given that the dollar was supposed to be "as good as gold," convertible on demand), some countries, notably France, were beginning to doubt the long-term viability of a system that substituted green pieces of paper for gold.

U.S. gold reserves fell from a high of $25 billion in 1950 to $10 billion in 1970. During the same period foreign dollar claims against the U.S. gold supply increased from around $5 billion to $70 billion. Clearly it no longer made sense to say that the dollar was convertible to gold on demand since the potential dollar claims against the U.S. gold supply were seven times larger than could be honored.

Faced with a building crisis of confidence President Nixon cut the link between the dollar and gold on August 15, 1971. The United States would no longer honor its pledge to redeem dollars for gold. This meant that the rest of the world was left holding $70 billion that were worth only what the U.S. government said they were worth. Surprisingly most foreign governments accepted this as an inevitable reality and continued to use dollars as reserves and as the international medium of exchange. There was no alternative. This was the final step in establishing that the international financial system was based on dollars. Gold eventually became just another commodity, which could be bought and sold on the commodity markets at whatever price it would bring.

By the end of 1971, the United States was experiencing a major balance-of-payments problem. Its current account deficit had grown to a deficit of $1.4 billion, and the trade deficit had reached an unprecedented $2.2 billion. The Nixon administration responded to this situation on December 18, 1971, by initiating the historic Smithsonian Agreement, which formalized the results of President Nixon's New Economic Policy (NEP). The NEP, in addition to halting the convertibility of the dollar into gold, provided for a 10 percent tax on the value of all imports and the floating of the dollar. In effect, the United States would neither buy nor sell currency on the foreign exchange markets. Exchange rates would be left to determine their own level or be influenced by the intervention of other governments. Floating the dollar and cutting its link to gold violated the established operational guidelines of the IMF. In essence, the Smithsonian Agreement represented the collapse of the Bretton Woods system.

Petrodollar Recycling

By 1973 the dollar was firmly entrenched as the world's key international currency, and the stage was set for the beginning of the most serious crisis ever faced by the international monetary system. Interestingly what happened was as much a political problem as it was an economic one.

Outraged by the U.S. support of Israel during the Yom Kippur War, the Organization of Petroleum Exporting Countries (OPEC), which had gained a dominant position in the world oil market by the early 1970s, placed an embargo on oil sales to the United States. Later, when that was relaxed, OPEC dramatically raised the price of oil (from $1.30 a barrel in 1970 to $10.72 by 1975). Since most oil transactions are carried out in dollars and because, at the time, the United States was dependent on OPEC for almost 50 percent of its oil imports, this sent an inflationary shock through the U.S. economy and the rest of the world.

Having no short-run alternative, the United States and the rest of the world paid the price. A result of the OPEC price increase was one of the most massive transfers of wealth in history. Hundreds of billions of dollars were transferred from oil-consuming nations to the Middle Eastern oil-producing countries. The OPEC nations were then faced with the ironic and paradoxical problem of what to do with this windfall. Clearly their own economies could not absorb such an injection of funds without risking runaway inflation. They had no alternative but to look for other places to invest them.

In spite of the problems caused by the oil shock, the United States economy was still the strongest in the world. The only logical step for the dollar-rich OPEC nations was to cycle the oil revenues back into U.S. and European banks. By 1976 the OPEC countries had placed nearly $100 billion in deposits in these banks, which now were faced with a paradoxical dilemma: billions of new dollar deposits and, with a recession (caused in part by the higher oil prices) going on in the United States, nowhere to put them to work. Since banks must pay interest on deposits, it follows that they can survive only if they are able to loan out those deposits at higher rates than they have to pay depositors. Within the ramifications of this elementary fact are the roots of the present economic crisis.

Most Third World countries were desperate for outside development capital, especially since most of them are also dependent on oil imports and were, along with the industrialized nations, forced to pay the higher oil prices. Therefore they were prime candidates for loans from U.S. and European commercial banks. In what seemed to many to be a logical process at the time (capital moving to where it is needed), the underdeveloped countries were only too willing to absorb the banks' excess funds. Everybody was happy. Bankers lined up at the doors of finance ministers' offices with loan money in hand. And the cycle was complete. Almost.

The process, now called petrodollar recycling, involved the Middle Eastern countries' shipping the oil to the United States and Europe, which, in turn, had sent along the dollars to pay for it to the Middle East (figure 1–2). The OPEC countries then deposited those same dollars back in U.S. and European banks, which in turn loaned them to the capital-poor Third World countries. Unfortunately, as everyone now knows (in hindsight), this is where the cycle stopped and where the seeds of the present debt crisis were planted.

The Oil Shock of 1973–1974

The system of floating exchange rates was challenged by the shock of the 1973–1974 OPEC oil embargo. The dramatic rise in oil prices severely disrupted the international monetary system; nevertheless, the recycling of petrodollars took place without the catastrophic disruption and disequilibrium that many experts had predicted.

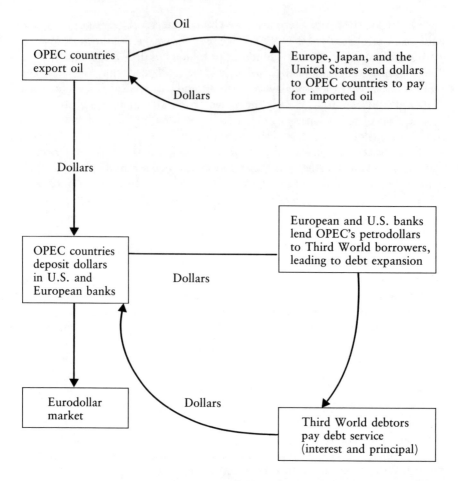

Figure 1–2. OPEC Petrodollar Recycling

By the middle of the 1970s chronic balance-of-payments problems plagued most developing nations, particularly those that needed to import oil. These balance-of-payments deficits placed greater and greater pressure upon the IMF for adjustment loans and assistance, and it was rapidly becoming clear that the organization was increasingly being called on to perform a function never intended when it was created. At its inception, the IMF was organized only to assist nations with temporary short-run balance-of-payments problems and economic stabilization. Now it was confronting much more serious problems.

These chronic balance-of-payment deficits reflected the long-festering structural problems of the Third World. Most developing nations were facing a constant deterioration of their terms of trade and an outflow of capital to pay for their oil and other badly needed imports. They needed even more new loans to pay for oil imports and to adjust to declining export revenues caused by the U.S. recession of 1974–1975, another by-product of the oil price shock. The general interdependence of the industrialized world and the underdeveloped nations was becoming increasingly clear.

The increasing collective consciousness of the nonaligned developing nations in the late 1960s and early 1970s produced extensive debate, with dialogue centering on the need for a global restructuring of the international economic and financial systems. These discussions resulted in the Sixth Special Session of the United Nations in April 1974, when two resolutions were drafted and adopted. The first called for the establishment of a New International Economic Order (NIEO). The second outlined the Programme of Action to bring it about. With these actions, the Group of 77 (the developing nations) evidenced a new global posture, substituting "defiance for the deference of the past."

On December 12, 1974, at the regularly scheduled Twenty-ninth Session of the U.N. General Assembly, the call for an NIEO was reaffirmed in the adoption of the Charter of Economic Rights and Duties of States. In 1975, the United Nations called for the "full and complete economic emancipation" of the developing world. The Declaration of the U.N. General Assembly on the Establishment of a New International Economic Order, stated in part:

> We, the Members of the United Nations,
> Having convened a special session of the General Assembly to study for the first time the problems of raw materials and development, . . .
> Solemnly proclaim our united determination to work urgently for THE ESTABLISHMENT OF A NEW INTERNATIONAL ECONOMIC ORDER based on equity, sovereign equality, interdependence, common interest and co-operation among all States, irrespective of their economic and social systems which shall correct inequalities and redress existing injustices, make it possible to eliminate the widening gap between the developed and the developing countries and ensure steadily accelerating economic and social development and peace and justice for present and future generations, and, to that end, declare:
> 1. The greatest and most significant achievement during the last decades has been the independence from colonial and alien domination of a large number of peoples and nations which has enabled them to become members of the community of free peoples. Technological progress has also been made in all spheres of economic activities in the last three decades, thus providing a solid potential for improving the well-being of all peoples. However, the remaining vestiges of alien and colonial domination, foreign occupation, racial discrimination, apartheid and neo-colonialism in all its forms continue to be among the greatest obstacles to the full emancipation and progress of the developing countries and all the peoples involved. The benefits of technological progress are not shared equitably by all members of the international community. The developing countries, which constitute 70 percent of the world's population, account for only 30 percent of the world's income. It has proved

impossible to achieve an even and balanced development of the international community under the existing international economic order. The gap between the developed and the developing countries continues to widen in a system which was established at a time when most of the developing countries did not even exist as independent States and which perpetuates inequality.

2. The present international economic order is in direct conflict with current developments in international political and economic relations. Since 1970, the world economy has experienced a series of grave crises which have had severe repercussions, especially on the developing countries because of their generally greater vulnerability to external economic impulses. The developing world has become a powerful factor that makes its influence felt in all fields of international activity. These irreversible changes in the relationship of forces in the world necessitate the active, full and equal participation of the developing countries in the formulation and application of all decisions that concern the international community.

3. All these changes have thrust into prominence the reality of interdependence of all the members of the world community. Current events have brought into sharp focus the realization that the interests of the developed countries and those of the developing countries can no longer be isolated from each other, that there is a close interrelationship between the prosperity of the developing countries and the growth and development of the developing countries, and that the prosperity of the international community as a whole depends upon the prosperity of its constituent parts. International co-operation for development is the shared goal and common duty of all countries. Thus the political, economic and social well-being of present and future generations depends more than ever on co-operation between all the members of the international community on the basis of sovereign equality and the removal of the dis-equilibrium that exists between them.[2]

These words, now long-forgotten, were much more prophetic than anyone realized at the time.

The International Monetary Fund

In order to qualify for a trade adjustment loan from the IMF, a country is usually required to agree to a set of economic policies judged by the IMF to be appropriate for stabilizing the economy and eliminating what it determines to be the causes of the country's balance-of-payments problems. Quite often the IMF's economic stabilization package requires the country to adopt an austerity program that includes measures to reduce imports and increase exports, currency devaluation, reduction in government spending, tax increases to reduce the rate of inflation, and policies designed to attract more foreign investment. These economic policy measures are generally meant to result in a period of declining economic growth and austerity. Usually the understanding between the IMF and the borrowing country was that some short-term sacrifice was necessary to restore long-term economic growth and stability. But while a country's governmental officials may have understood this, such policies were not popular with the majority of citizens, who had to pay the price of a reduced standard of living.

The economic chaos of the Carter years exacerbated the situation seriously as it set the stage for higher interest rates and a precipitous increase in debt servicing costs. A second round of OPEC price increases sent the U.S. economy into a three-year period of stagflation (1979–1981). The oil price increase brought higher interest rates and soaring inflation coupled with declining economic growth and increasing rates of unemployment. Moreover, the oil import bills of all industrialized nations increased, as did those of the oil-importing developing nations. And OPEC, once again, was faced with the financial challenge of prudently allocating oil revenues for internal development and investing the surplus in European and U.S. banks and government securities.

At the same time, as a consequence of the higher oil prices (and many other factors, such as declining trade, spiraling inflation, compounding past loans, and rising interest rates), the oil-dependent developing nations increased their demand for loans from the IMF and now, more important, from private commercial banks. Because the IMF's limited loan capability was not sufficient to meet the avalanche of credit demand, private commercial banks eagerly stepped in to fill the gap. Flush with petrodollar deposits and facing limited demand for credit in their own countries because of the prolonged recession, the banks were only too happy to oblige. Because of tight U.S. monetary policy, interest rates were at record highs, so bankers faced the pleasant prospect of making and often encouraging what they thought would be extremely profitable loans to developing nations with what appeared to be little risk.

Emergence of the Strong Dollar Syndrome

The new policy prescriptions of the Reagan administration were to have far-reaching consequences for the international financial system in general and the debt crisis in particular. Reagan had campaigned on a platform of supply-side economics. His goals were to reduce taxes and government spending on domestic programs. According to supply-side theories, this policy mix would generate a burst of economic growth and output sufficient to reduce inflation, decrease unemployment, and balance the budget all at the same time. In addition, Reaganomics emphasized the continuation of free floating exchange rates and strongly supported free trade, though the U.S. trade deficit was growing worse.

The supply-side economic program was accompanied by a tight monetary policy on the part of the Federal Reserve Bank between 1981 and 1983, which induced the worst recession since the 1930s. It finally broke the back of inflation—but at a high social and economic price: two years of severe unemployment, declining economic growth, a record-high federal budget deficit, and an increasing balance-of-trade deficit.

By 1982 the U.S. economy had begun to recover, but the seeds of crisis had been sown. The high interest rates of this period strengthened the U.S. dollar once again as foreign investment flowed in seeking the higher returns, but this was to have far-reaching implications. Most important, the strong dollar directly made the U.S. trade deficit even worse as it made U.S. exports more expensive and imports cheaper (table 1–1).

For the developing nations, the continued high level of interest rates made their annual trek to the bank and the IMF even more expensive. Their balance-of-payments problems were exacerbated by a further slowdown in world trade and economic growth, which caused their exports and foreign exchange earnings to fall precipitously.

In 1978 there was a capital outflow to the Third World countries from the industrialized nations of $37.5 billion. But the situation began to deteriorate rapidly in the early 1980s, and by 1984 there was a net drain (an inflow in the capital account) of $34.6 billion. This was mostly due to a sharp reduction in new bank loans to the underdeveloped countries, while interest and principal amortization payment obligations continued. In 1982, at the depth of the U.S. recession when both interest rates and oil prices were still high, the current account deficit—balance of trade plus investment income flows—reached a crushing $90 billion. By then it was becoming obvious that the Third World debt situation was reaching crisis proportions. However, it took a near collapse of the Mexican economy to bring the problem to world attention.

Table 1–1
U.S. Trade Deficit, 1977–1987

Year	Trade Deficit (billions)
1977	$ − 31.0
1978	− 33.9
1979	− 27.5
1980	− 25.5
1981	− 29.9
1982	− 36.4
1983	− 67.2
1984	− 114.1
1985	− 150.0
1986	− 170.0
1987	− 160.0

Source: *Economic Report of the President* (Washington, D.C.: Government Printing Office, 1988).

The Mexican Crisis of 1982

On Friday August 13, 1982, Mexican finance minister Jesus Silva-Herzog arrived in Washington with what amounted to a bombshell: Mexico was bankrupt. It owed $81 billion in foreign debts—$68 billion of that to commercial banks—and could not pay even the interest on its obligations. It needed an immediate loan of $3 billion just to cover interest payments coming due in August and September. Later it would need more, he informed the startled monetary authorities at the U.S. Treasury and the Federal Reserve Bank. Otherwise Mexico would be forced to default.

A default by Mexico would have meant losses of around $12 billion for the six largest U.S. banks. That alone would have reduced the value of their capital (shareholders' equity) by almost 50 percent, and it would severely damage all of the 1,400 U.S. banks with loans out to Mexico. Citicorp, the largest U.S. bank, would lose more than $3 billion—two-thirds of its capital. A crisis of this magnitude would put strains on the international financial system far beyond what the U.S. government could allow. It was not Mexico that was in trouble; it was the United States. The old saying, "If you owe a bank a thousand dollars and can't pay, you're in trouble. But if you owe a bank a million dollars and can't pay, the bank is in trouble," had turned out to be all too true.

The U.S. monetary authorities, under the leadership of Paul Volcker, quickly put together a rescue loan package that temporarily averted total collapse. The package was made up of a $1 billion advance payment by the Department of Energy for oil destined for the U.S. strategic petroleum reserve, $1 billion from the Department of Agriculture, $700 million from the Federal Reserve Bank, and $300 million from the U.S. Treasury in the form of a currency swap arrangement. Later Mexico got an additional $1.85 billion line of credit from the Bank of International Settlements and, with unprecedented rapidity, almost $4 billion from the IMF—on the condition that the commercial banks cough up an additional $5 billion, which they did reluctantly. By December the rescue package was completed: Mexico had borrowed enough to meet its immediate obligation. But in the process, it ended up some $14 billion further in debt. The phrase *Third World debt crisis* had become part of the national lexicon.

Mexico's debt crisis focused worldwide attention on an international financial problem that had been brewing for many years, but few had been willing to acknowledge its magnitude until it reached the crisis stage. Now the global debt crisis was added to the seemingly unending list of global economic problems. But the major Western governments were so preoccupied with their own stagnating economies that they did not confront the wide-ranging, long-run implications of the crisis. It suddenly became clear that not only Mexico was in trouble; so were Argentina, Brazil, Chile, Venezuela, Peru, Nigeria, the Philippines, Turkey, Poland, Romania, and many others—most of the underdeveloped world.

The Reagan administration's response was to facilitate the extension of additional loans by the IMF and private commercial banks to enable the debtor countries to continue meeting their obligations with borrowed money. If this meant they would face domestic economic austerity, then, the United States argued, that would be necessary until global economic growth and the recovery of the industrialized nations could improve the export capacity of developing nations.

The expected recovery did come in 1983. By 1984 world trade had expanded at an annual rate of 8.5 percent, and world output grew at an annual rate of 4.2 percent. For developing nations, 1984 brought growth rates of 4.1 percent and an increase in exports of 8.0 percent, compared to only 4 percent two years earlier. But even with this recovery, which continued into 1985, it became obvious that the international economic problems were not going to go away. Part of the problem was the continued strong dollar and the free-flexible exchange rate system.

The Plaza Agreement of 1985

At the initiative of treasury secretary James Baker III, the United States invited the five largest industrial nations (United States, Great Britain, France, West Germany, and Japan) to New York to discuss the exchange rate problem. At this meeting, held at the Plaza Hotel in September 1985, this Group of 5 agreed to return to an informal system of managed exchange rates. Yet in spite of the so-called Plaza Agreement, the major problems—the U.S. trade deficit and the huge Third World debt—remained and were two of the primary issues on the agenda of the Tokyo Economic Summit in May 1986. There were other problems too: the pace of industrial world growth, the direction of the U.S. dollar, the possibility of policy coordination, high interest rates, and the U.S. federal budget deficit.

Overall world industrial growth was increasing, but most participants continued to express concern over the slowing of economic growth in the United States. The Reagan administration took the position that Japan and West Germany should stimulate their economies to spend up their economic growth rates to increase their demand for imports, especially U.S. exports. Japan and West Germany did not agree; they felt such stimulation would be excessively inflationary.

The major issue at the Tokyo Summit was that of policy coordination. Since each nation's economy had started to converge (declining interest rates, real growth continuing, and lower inflation), it was possible to begin thinking seriously about coordinating economic policies. But since unemployment rates and trade deficits varied considerably in each country, the prospects for workable economy policy coordination appeared to be remote, and there was no formal agreement. The summit participants did, however, acknowledge that another year had gone by without a Third World debt crisis (except for the unique case of Mexico). Declining interest rates and oil prices had brought an easing of the debt problem for most developing nations. And the summit group endorsed a plan developed by Treasury Secretary James Baker III to aid debtor countries by generating an additional $29 billion in loans from the IMF and the World Bank ($9 billion) and private commercial banks ($20 billion), to be spread among seventeen countries.

At the conclusion of the Tokyo Summit, there appeared to be a renewed spirit of cooperation and a determination to work toward a more cooperative and coordinated set of economic policies that would simultaneously promote and protect the interests of each individual nation while considering the consequences and ramifications on the group as a whole. But except for some coordinated interest rate reductions, little was accomplished at that meeting. There was, however, general agreement that the U.S. dollar was "too strong" and that something should be done. Therefore in a historically significant departure from the free-flexible exchange rate system that had prevailed since the Nixon administration, the Group of 5 (G-5) industrialized nations agreed to intervene in the exchange markets to bring the value of the dollar down. They were successful. This was a tacit recognition that the huge U.S. trade deficit was one of the major international economic roadblocks to solving the imbalance of trade problem.

Reducing the value of the dollar, the G-5 leaders felt, would make U.S. exports cheaper and the price of imports higher, thus eventually reducing the U.S. balance-of-trade deficit. The dollar fell by 40 percent against the yen over a six-month period beginning in September 1985. By the spring of 1986 it was at the lowest level it had been since 1947—140 yen to the dollar. But the trade deficit did not budge, defying a long-standing economic theory, and the international economists went back to the drawing boards.

What is supposed to happen in such a devaluation is that a so-called J curve effect takes place. At first, because imports suddenly become more expensive in dollar terms, the trade balance gets worse. But soon imports decline and exports increase, and trade is brought back into balance. For a number of complicated reasons, this did not happen. Partly the dollar was not strong for the reason it normally would have been (because of a strong international trade position). Instead it was strong because a huge sum of foreign investment money was flowing into the United States seeking "safe haven" investments and because of the high rates of return available because of high interest rates in the United States compared to the rest of the world. Devaluing the dollar did not change that situation significantly.

Beyond that, while the dollar did fall against some U.S. trading partners, such as Japan and West Germany, it did not fall against others, notably Canada, Mexico, and especially against the increasingly important NICs such as Taiwan,

South Korea, and the Pacific rim countries that tie their currences to the value of the dollar. In addition, U.S. demand for imports appears to be insatiable because most Americans seem to have become convinced that foreign-made products are superior in quality to U.S. products.

As a consequence, in spite of the fall of the dollar, the U.S. trade deficit did not improve. It exceeded $156 billion in 1986 and was $174 in 1987. And it was a major agenda item on the Venice Economic Summit in June 1987.

The Venice Summit

In a climate of having to bail Mexico out of another debt-servicing crisis in 1986, only to be faced with a moratorium by Brazil—the largest Third World debtor—on most of its foreign debt, continued high U.S. budget and trade deficits, and a U.S. president weakened by the Iran-contra scandal, the leaders of the seven largest industrial nations met once again in Venice to try to resolve the continuing economic chaos. Their communiqué declared:

> We, the heads of state or government of the seven major industrialized countries and the representatives of the European Community, have met in Venice from 8 to 10 June 1987, to review the progress that our countries have made, individually and collectively, in carrying out the policies to which we committed ourselves at earlier summits. We remain determined to pursue these policies for growth, stability, employment, and prosperity for our countries and for the world economy.
>
> We can look back on a number of positive developments since we met a year ago. Growth is continuing into its fifth consecutive year, albeit at lower rates. Average inflation rates have come down. Interest rates have generally declined. Changes have occurred in relationships among leading currencies which over time will contribute to a more sustainable pattern of current account positions and have brought exchange rates within ranges broadly consistent with economic fundamentals. In volume terms the adjustment of trade flows is under way, although in nominal terms imbalances so far remain too large. . . .
>
> We now need to overcome the problems that nevertheless remain in some of our countries: external imbalances that are still large; persistently high unemployment; large public sector deficits; and high levels of real interest rates. There are also continuing trade restrictions and increased protectionist pressures, persistent weakness of many primary commodity markets, and reduced prospects for developing countries to grow, find the markets they need and service their foreign debt.
>
> The correction of external imbalances will be a long and difficult process. Exchange rate changes alone will not solve the problem of correcting these imbalances while sustaining growth. Surplus countries will design their policies to strengthen domestic demand and reduce external surpluses while maintaining price stability. Deficit countries, while following policies designed to encourage steady low-inflation growth, will reduce their fiscal and external imbalances. . . .

We also agree on the need for effective structural policies especially for creating jobs. To this end we shall:

—Promote competition in order to speed up industrial adjustment;

—Reduce major imbalances between agricultural supply and demand;

—Facilitate job creating investment;

—Improve the functioning of labor markets;

—Promote the further opening of internal markets;

—Encourage the elimination of capital markets imperfections and restrictions and the improvement of the functioning of international financial markets. . . .

We note rising protectionist pressures with grave concern. . . . Recognizing the interrelationship among growth, trade and development, it is essential to improve the multilateral system based on the principles and rules of the General Agreement on Tariffs and Trade and bring about a wider coverage of world trade under agreed, effective and enforceable multilateral discipline. Protectionist actions would be counterproductive, would increase the risk of further exchange rate instability and would exacerbate the problems of development and indebtedness. . . .

We attach particular importance to fostering stable economic progress in developing countries, with all their diverse situations and needs. The problems of many heavily indebted developing countries are a cause of economic and political concern and can be a threat to political stability in countries with democratic regimes. We salute the courageous efforts of many of these countries to achieve economic growth and stability.

We underline the continuing importance of official development assistance. . . .

—We support the central role of the I.M.F. through its advice and financing and encourage closer cooperation between the I.M.F. and the World Bank, especially in their structural adjustment lending. . . .

—We support a general capital increase of the World Bank. . . .

—In the light of the different contributions of our countries to official development assistance, we welcome the recent initiative of the Japanese Government in bringing forward a new scheme which will increase the provision of resources from Japan to developing countries.

For the major middle-income debtors, we continue to support the present growth-oriented case-by-case strategy. . . .

There is equally a need for timely and effective mobilization of lending by commercial banks. In this context, we support efforts by commercial banks and debtor countries to develop a "menu" of alternative negotiating procedures and financial techniques for providing continuing support to debtor countries. . . .

We recognize the problems of developing countries whose economies are soley or predominantly dependent on exports of primary commodities the prices of which are persistently depressed. It is important that the functioning of commodity markets should be improved. . . .

We note that UNCTAD VII provides an opportunity for a discussion with developing countries with a view to arriving at a common perception of the major problems and policy issues in the world economy.[3]

On the surface the joint communiqué seemed impressive. The public acknowledgment of the need for better coordination of economic policies, the recognition that the problem of Third World debt must be resolved, and the need to address trade imbalances seemed to point to an action-oriented solution. But in fact, almost nothing at all happened at or after the Venice Summit. What did not happen is more significant than what did.

Most important, what did not happen is that no one was ready to acknowledge that the United States no longer enjoys hegemony over the world economy and instead, has become a prisoner of international economic forces that now seem far beyond its control. But the dollar remains the linchpin currency, used in more than 50 percent of all international transactions. That situation cannot continue. A new system, consistent with the present realities of the modern world, must be put in place. The Venice Summit did not recognize this need. It simply endorsed trial-and-error muddle-along efforts that are clearly not working.

Its first proposal was to reduce the U.S. budget deficit, which is supposed to somehow magically solve all the world's problems. But there is no evidence to indicate that the deficit can be reduced in the foreseeable future, and even if it is, there is no reason to think that this solution alone will solve the problem of structural trade imbalance. And, in any case, President Reagan's response to those proposals was that the United States is already doing all it can to reduce its deficit.

Second, Japan, West Germany, and the other European countries were encouraged to stimulate their economies on the assumption that their faster growth would absorb more U.S. exports. But growth rates in those countries are nearly stagnant and showing no signs of improvement. Moreover, there are no signs that anyone wants to do anything about it. But even if they did, there is no evidence that faster growth would resolve the longer-run festering problems. Several studies show that even a 1 percent growth rate increase in Japan and West Germany would improve the U.S. trade deficit by only 25 percent over a five-year period.

Third, it was generally recognized that the United States needs to become more competitive in world markets, but the United States—still the most productive economy in the world—has become more competitive in terms of output per man-hour, especially in the manufacturing sector where productivity increased at a rate of 2.6 percent in the first half of 1987, but U.S. exports have hardly increased at all, and even if they did, that would not resolve the longer-run problem unless imports—which have remained constant—were cut back drastically.

Fourth, there was agreement that the value of the dollar should be reduced, or at least maintained at the lower levels achieved by central bank interventions after the Plaza Agreement in 1985. But by the end of 1987 the lower value of the dollar had not improved the U.S. trade deficit at all and, if it did, the risk of a systemic collapse would be greatly increased. A lower dollar exchange rate would increase the price of U.S. imports even more and put inflationary pressures on the economy that would force the monetary authorities to increase interest rates, tighten the money supply, or both. That, in turn would push the economy into a recession, which would reverberate throughout the world.

A weaker dollar also means lower rates of return for foreign investors as their dollar-denominated investments translate into smaller rates of return in terms of their home country currencies. That means that the risk of a foreign investment pullout is greatly increased. If that happened, a dollar collapse or a dollar panic would be inevitable. So simply depreciating the value of the dollar is not a viable short-run or long-run solution. It is, at best, a delicate balancing act between possible chaos on the one hand and recession on the other.

Fifth, there was general agreement that protectionist legislation, especially in the United States, should be avoided at all costs, and the G-7 industrialized nations recommitted themselves, rhetorically at least, to the continuing General Agreement on Tariffs and Trade (GATT) negotiations to reduce tariffs and import quotas. But even if all trade restrictions were removed, it is estimated that the U.S. trade deficit would not improve by more than 3 percent. Beyond that, the Omnibus Trade Bill, which became law in 1988, was the most protectionist trade legislation passed by the U.S. Congress since 1932. Talking about reduction of trade barriers has a hollow ring. Free trade is an attractive theory but an unlikely reality.

Finally, the Third World debt crisis, which has been worsening at an increasing rate, was hardly discussed, although there was some acknowledgment that the impoverished nations of Africa need some special attention.

Interestingly, the one significant agreement by the Venice Summit was largely unnoticed in the press: the Group of 7 agreed to adopt an international economic plan developed by their finance ministers during 1986. Treasury Secretary Baker announced that the nations would begin tracking their economies using a newly developed series of economic indicators and that when any member of the group begins to drift off course, the ministers would meet. What exactly these indicators are will be kept secret, but most likely they will include trade balance data, interest rates, budget projections, inflation and growth rates, and currency exchange rates.

This has not been done in the past because each nation has its own method of keeping track of these data so comparisons among countries are often meaningless. For example, because of the way it is defined, a cut in the Japanese or West German discount rate means much less than it does in the United States; unemployment rates are calculated differently; and so on. Parties to the new agreement will use the same system, and the results will be much more meaningful. The agreement, however, is nonbinding because no country will ever consent to a binding agreement that could subvert its control of its own economy. The only "automatic" mechanism is that the finance ministers did agree to meet any time when difficulties arose.

The Venice Summit, in sum, merely reaffirmed a set of anachronistic solutions that have been tried but have not worked economically and are not feasible politically. The world economy is in a period of transition that needs to be managed and coordinated in an orderly manner. It has become clear that the United States can no longer manage it to its own interests. A new system of coordination is badly needed and, to put it in place, a new conference on the order of Bretton Woods.

2
The Triple Debt Crisis

In the 1980s debt has come to dominate the news from every angle; it is no longer buried in the financial pages. The explosive growth of debt everywhere has become the economic issue of the decade. Indeed a triple debt crisis has evolved. First, the U.S. national federal debt exceeded $2.3 trillion in 1987, more than double what it was only five years earlier. Second, in the fall of 1985 the United States became a debtor nation for the first time since 1914. U.S. external debt reached $263 billion in 1987 and is expected to exceed $1 trillion by 1990. And third, in 1988 Third World debt to the industrialized countries stood at nearly $1 trillion. Most of Third World debt is owed to U.S. banks, which have publicly acknowledged that the chances they will be repaid are slim to nonexistent. Such a buildup of debt is historically unprecedented, and it has sown the seeds of a major crisis, if not a total collapse, of the international financial system.

Debt has always played a significant and important role in economics. It is often said that the real measure of one's wealth is "not how much you have but how much you can borrow." But in the American psyche, the word *debt* has a negative connotation. People are supposed to "save their money and live within their means." Nonetheless, people go into debt for a number of legitimate reasons: to buy a home or a car or to finance a college education. So long as one's income increases as fast as or faster than new debt does, there is no problem so long as the interest on the debt can be serviced. Indeed, managing debt properly is an important part of prudent financial planning. Debt is an integral part of the American way of life. Only when a household's debt begins to exceed its capacity to pay its interest and principal obligations is it in danger of bankruptcy.

Businesses too go into debt for legitimate reasons. They borrow to invest in expanding capacity, to finance inventories, to build new plants, and for a host of other reasons. Virtually all businesses depend on debt to operate. Clearly debt is not inherently negative in the context of prudent business mangement.

When a business goes into debt, there is a presumption that the rate of return generated by the investments made possible by borrowing will exceed the rate of interest on its loans. Thus, the earnings from the investment project will be more than sufficient to repay the money used to finance it. That is one of the reasons interest exists. Money—financial capital, it is called—is presumed to be productive in the sense that investing it creates a rate of return higher than the price of money, which is the interest rate. Otherwise banks would not exist. But when a business's debt exceeds its capacity to service it, it too is in trouble, and bankruptcy may eventually ensue.

As with households and businesses, so with the nations of the world. There are a variety of reasons for countries to go into debt: to finance needed defense expenditures, to invest in public works, and so on. But now the situation becomes a bit more complicated. Nations can go into debt in two different ways: by borrowing internally, from their own citizens, or by borrowing externally, from other nations. Either way can make economic sense; either can get out of control. The latter is what happened in the United States and most of the rest of the Western world in the 1980s.

The U.S. Debt and Deficits

The federal government's huge debt ranks high on everybody's list of economic concerns. Several polls conducted in 1988 showed that a majority of Americans thought the national debt was the country's biggest problem. And it may be, but for different reasons than most people think. There are two different ways of looking at the national debt question, and that gives rise to a lot of mythology as people attempt to sort it out using different assumptions, which we will call the *barnyard economics way* and the *economics of public finance way.*

Those who look at the federal debt from the barnyard perspective argue that it is not prudent for the government to spend more than it takes in. After all, if households and individuals cannot do it, why should the government be able to? But this view does not fit well with the facts because households and governments do not face the same reality. The reason households have to balance their budgets ("save their money and live within their means") is that although individuals may be able to spend more than they earn for short periods of time, that situation cannot go on very long. Also households must attempt to save for retirement, so prudent personal financial management makes sense. Since this is a process deeply ingrained in the American way of life, it is not surprising that many would extrapolate it to the government.

Governments, however, do not face the same fiscal restraints that households do. Governments can raise their incomes any time by increasing taxes. To be sure this may have other, less desirable, side effects, but it is possible—and very common. Also since governments, in theory at least, exist in perpetuity, they do not have the constraint of needing to save for retirement. In sum, governments do not have to manage their financial affairs in the same way that households do. The commonly drawn comparison is a fallacy.

A somewhat more sophisticated view of the national debt issue—the public finance economist's view—described in virtually every elementary economics textbook, argues that the national debt is not a problem at all. The chief reason is that there is a lot of confusion over the question of who owes what to whom. The national debt consists of the total of all U.S. Treasury bills, notes, and bonds outstanding at any time. When the government runs a deficit, spending more than it takes in from taxes and other sources, that amount is added to the national debt as additional securities are issued and sold. In 1987 the total amount of such securities outstanding (the national debt) was roughly $2.3 trillion. The relevant and commonly misunderstood question here is: Who owns these interest-bearing assets? That is, to whom does the government owe this money? The interesting answer is that, in one way or another, most of it is owed to U.S. citizens. Anyone who owns a U.S. savings bond or any other kind of U.S. government security owns part of the national debt. So who owes whom? For the most part, the government owes the debt to its own citizens, who not only own it but receive interest payments on it.

Moreover, a large part of the national debt is owned by the government itself or by quasi-governmental agencies. The U.S. central bank—the Federal Reserve system—owned $230 billion of U.S. Treasury obligations in 1986. The social security trusts held $390 billion. Together these two quasi-governmental institutions held 27 percent of the total debt. So the net debt outside the government itself was only around $1.7 trillion rather than the more publicized $2.3 trillion. Much of the rest of the debt is owned by banks (27 percent), insurance companies (7 percent), state and local governments (11 percent), and other institutions. Only 9 percent is owned by individuals directly (figure 2–1).

The other reason that most economists have tended to downplay the importance of the federal debt is that historically both the economy and the government's income have grown much faster than the debt. They point out that as a percentage of national income, the debt has been getting smaller and smaller. So in that context, it has become a decreasing burden on the government. That was indeed the case, at least until 1980 (figure 2–2).

In 1946 the national debt, mostly accumulated during the war, stood at 127 percent of the U.S. GNP. By 1986 that percentage had dropped to 54 and, if the Federal Reserve and social security holdings are netted out, the debt was only 36 percent of the country's GNP that year—clearly high, but even by household comparisons not overwhelming. If anything, rather than hindering economic growth and general prosperity, as some would argue, the debt has probably stimulated it. So put in that context the national debt, many economists feel, is not a serious problem.

That has been the conventional wisdom in economics for some time. But it is becoming more apparent that the U.S. economy may have bitten off a lot more debt than it can chew. Three new developments are causing even liberal economists and politicians to reevaluate their position on the national debt: interest payments, compounding, and the growing federal deficits.

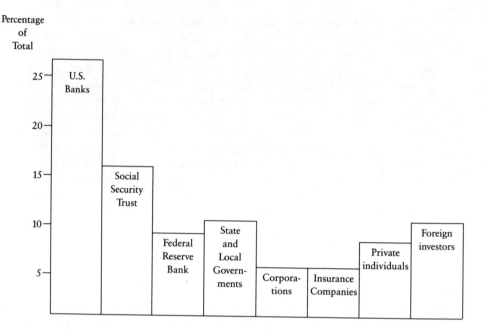

Source: *Economic Report of the President* (Washington, D.C.: Government Printing Office, 1987).
Note: In 1986 total U.S. public debt was $2.3 trillion.

Figure 2–1. Ownership of U.S. National Debt, 1986

Interest Payments

In 1976 net interest payments—the difference between what the government pays out in interest and what it takes in—were $26.8 billion, or 6.8 percent of federal expenditures. In 1986 the federal government made net interest payments of $135.8 billion, or 13.2 percent of federal expenditures. Interest payments on the debt are now the third largest category in the budget, after national defense and social security. They are causing a massive transfer of wealth from the middle class, which pays most of the taxes, to the wealthy, who own most of the government debt. This is becoming an increasingly serious problem, especially considering that the top 20 percent of income receivers already receive 45 percent of all income, while the bottom 20 percent get only 5 percent.

Compounding

Perhaps even more significant is the seemingly overlooked phenomenon of compounding. If money is left in the bank so the interest accumulates, savings will

% GNP

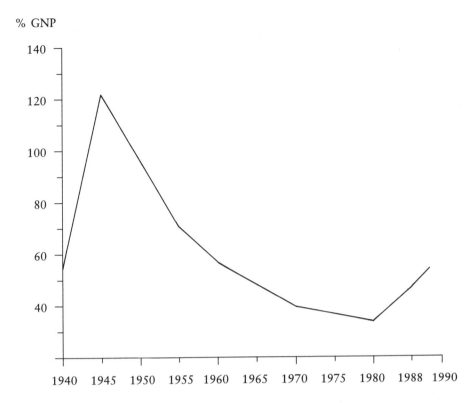

Source: Congressional Budget Office, *The Economic and Budget Outlook: Fiscal Years 1989–1993*, February 1988.

Figure 2–2. Federal Debt as a Percentage of GNP, 1940–1990

grow at a compound rate. At a 7 percent annual interest rate, they will double every ten years. By the same token, if money is borrowed to pay interest on what is owed, a similar compounding process occurs. That is what is happening to the U.S. national debt.

What is important here is the relationship between the growth of the national income and the growth of the debt. As with a household, if income grows as fast as debt, there is no problem; the debt can be serviced with no decline in living standards. That is what happened in the United States until around 1980. It is not happening now, and there is no reason to expect that it ever will again. Since 1980 the U.S. national debt has more than doubled, while the economy has grown by only 56 percent (and much less if the data are adjusted for inflation). If one makes only conservative assumptions and extrapolates a bit into the future, the numbers defy the imagination. Economist

Alfred Malabre has estimated that at current rates of growth, the U.S. national debt could reach $34 trillion by the year 2010.[1]

Federal Deficits

There is little evidence that the federal debt position can be improved unless drastic and politically unpopular tax increases are implemented.

The Reagan administration came into office on a campaign pledge to cut government spending, balance the federal budget, and reduce the national debt. Normally that would mean cutting spending and increasing taxes. Instead the administration chose to adopt a new version of an old theory called supply-side economics, the rationale of which was that if the burden of high marginal taxes is taken off the backs of individuals and businesses, they will work harder and save and invest more. This renewed burst of economic activity, the argument goes, will so stimulate the economy that (contrary to common sense) soon the tax decrease will cause an increase in governmental tax revenues.

One result of this peculiar variation on the idea of having your cake and eating it too was that the wealthy paid less in taxes but decided to spend their extra money rather than save it or invest it productively. By 1987 the national savings rate was running at less than 4 percent of disposable income, and investment had hardly increased. The other result of the tax decreases (in 1981 and again in 1986) was that federal deficits grew to record highs. Whenever the government runs a deficit, that amount is added to the national debt. The deficits grew from 40.2 billion in 1979 to $220 billion in 1986, and, as we have seen, the national debt more than doubled.

Moreover, because a large percentage of the federal budget goes either to defense spending or to entitlement programs, such as social security, federal pensions, and interest payments on the national debt itself, the administration was not successful in reducing government spending. In fact, the federal budget grew from $303 billion to under $1 trillion in 1986. Congressional efforts to cut spending were unsuccessful. The Gramm-Rudman law, which was to require a balanced budget, was declared unconstitutional by the Supreme Court and largely ignored in spirit by both the Congress and the administration, even after it was revised to meet constitutional requirements. The legacy of the Reagan administration and its ill-fated fantasies of supply-side economics is that the national debt has increased by more than the total accumulated debt of all previous administrations combined.

While it was once fashionable to argue that the national debt was not a serious problem, the realities of massive transfers of wealth from the poor to the rich and a runaway compounding of the debt to unimaginable heights means that the national debt problem is something the United States can no longer afford to ignore. The proverbial chickens have come home to roost.

Overall U.S. Debt Picture

The obvious gravity of the situation aside, in a sense the U.S. federal debt is a minor problem when it is put in the context of the growth of debt in the U.S. economy as a whole in the 1980s. Consider the following:

- Total personal, business, and governmental debt outstanding in the U.S. economy in 1987 exceeded $7 trillion—up $1 trillion from 1986.
- The ratio of total debt to the GNP stood at 1.7 in 1987, the highest since the 1930s. In 1981 the debt-GNP ratio was only 1.4.
- In 1987 corporate debt as a percentage of net worth grew to 120 percent, compared to 96 percent as recently as 1983.
- Utility and industrial corporations are so heavily leveraged that by 1987 there were only twenty-seven left in the entire country that merited the top AAA rating. Ten years earlier there were fifty-six.
- Although the economy in general was doing relatively well in 1986, some 138 banks—staggering under nonperforming agricultural and oil-based debts—failed. That is compared to only 42 in 1982 and more than in 1933 at the height of the Great Depression.
- In 1987 there were 1,500 banks on the Federal Deposit Insurance Corporation's problem bank list, up from 1,150 a year earlier.
- Household debt as a percentage of disposable income was, in 1987, just over 31 percent, compared to 25 percent in 1983.
- Personal bankruptcy filings climbed to a record 567,000 during the fiscal year ending June 30, 1986—a 35 percent increase over the previous year.
- The percentage of home mortgages being foreclosed doubled between 1982 and 1986 to a postwar high: one out of a hundred outstanding.

Total consumer debt (including home mortgages) exceeded $2 trillion by 1987 and has been growing at over 9 percent annually since 1980. That figure is around $24,000 for each of the 85 million households in the country. Consumer installment purchases alone in 1987 ran at almost 17 percent of personal income, compared to 12 percent in 1982.

Business debt, which now also exceeds $2 trillion, has been growing even faster—at a rate of almost 10 percent annually since 1984, compared to an average of 2.7 percent over the 1975–1983 period. Corporate debt now exceeds total corporate net worth by 12 percent.

What is more, the nature of corporate debt has been changing dramatically. Corporations have traditionally raised capital by issuing stock to the public, but in the past ten years, they have increasingly turned to banks and to issuing bonds instead. Bank loans as a percentage of total corporate external fund sources have increased from 22 percent in 1975 to almost 38 percent now, and bonds as a source of borrowing have grown from 34 percent to 45 percent over the same period. Direct debt has largely replaced equity (ownership) financing as a means for corporations to raise funds externally, and the cost of repaying these debts is now taking almost 20 percent of total corporate cash flow.

Such a buildup of the debt pyramid is almost unprecedented in U.S. economic history. Yet amid the euphoria of a rising stock market, it was largely ignored. In the five years of steady, albeit sluggish, economic growth of the U.S. economy between 1982 and 1987, the stock market (as measured by the Dow Jones average) grew by almost 250 percent, while the economy grew at only a 20 percent inflation-adjusted rate. The only parallel is the 1920s, when the market, built on a pyramid of credit, grew by 500 percent between 1921 and 1929, until it finally collapsed, taking the U.S. economy and the economies of the other Western nations with it into the Great Depression.[2]

In October 1987 the stock market collapsed. The Dow Jones average dropped 508 points in one day, and it became clear that the unfettered and unwarranted growth of the market was over. Many analysts predicted a severe recession would follow, but to nearly everyone's surprise, the economy continued to grow, albeit slowly, and while the market never recovered its dizzying heights, it ended 1987 slightly higher than it had been a year earlier.

Whether the debt bubble will ever burst, no one knows. But the implications of the debt explosion in the U.S. domestic economy pale by comparison to the developing international debt crisis. Largely as a result of its growing internal debt, the United States has now become a debtor nation externally. The long-run implications of that are much more serious than even the alarming domestic debt buildup.

It makes economic sense for a nation to borrow from abroad if the funds are used productively to develop its economy and, especially, its export capacity, so that the loans can be repaid. The United States borrowed heavily from Europe during the 1800s to finance the development of its industrial plant and westward expansion. Developing countries are, for the same reasons, usually debtor nations, and most economists agree that as a development strategy, this is prudent financial management if the loans are invested productively in manufacturing and needed infrastructure. Operating on those assumptions, the United States was a debtor nation until 1914. After that it began to show an export surplus, repaid the loans, and eventually became the world's largest creditor nation. U.S. export surpluses financed, among other things, the reconstruction of Europe after World War II, the expansion of U.S. investment worldwide, and the loaning of billions of dollars to the capital-poor Third World developing countries.

In the fall of 1985, that all changed dramatically when the United States became a debtor nation for the first time in seventy-one years. What this means is conceptually difficult to understand, but because it is crucial to understanding the nature and dimensions of the international financial crisis, it merits close examination.

There is a common misconception that if a nation consistently runs a balance-of-trade deficit, it is a debtor nation. In some cases that may be true, in others not. The confusion comes over the distinction between balance-of-trade transactions and overall balance-of-payments accounting.

By definition, the balance-of-payments accounts of a country must balance (as in double-entry bookeeping). It is possible for a country to run balance-of-trade deficits without becoming a debtor nation so long as there are off-setting transactions in the balance-of-payments accounts to make up for the excess of imports over exports. These can be sales of gold or accumulated foreign exchange, debits on special drawing rights from the IMF, net positive flows of income from foreign investments, or simply borrowing from other countries. Any of these financial transactions (and some others) will permit a country to import more than it exports. What counts in the long run is flows of capital investments as compared to the return flows of interest or profits from them.

The United States did not become a debtor nation because it went to Japan or Western Europe and "borrowed" money in the literal sense. Rather, what happened was that around 1983, the flow of capital into the United States from abroad—mostly from Japan and Western Europe—began to exceed the outflow of U.S. capital investments to the rest of the world. Historically the United States had counted on the net income from investments abroad to compensate for trade deficits and to help finance its military activities around the world.

U.S. net foreign investment income averaged $14.8 billion annually during the 1970s and peaked at over $34 billion in 1981. But after 1981 it began to decline rapidly as the rate of foreign investments in the United States began to grow at a faster rate than U.S. investments abroad. By 1987 U.S. net investment income had declined to $14.4 billion, and when netted with the huge balance of trade deficit (figure 2–3) the U.S. current account was a negative $160 billion at the end of 1987.

High interest rates resulting from the (successful) Volcker-Reagan effort to break the back of inflation, the general perception that the U.S. was a safe haven for investment, and the U.S. need for external savings to finance its own domestic national debt, coupled with huge Japanese and West German trade surpluses, added up to large increases in the flow of investment funds into the United States. The result was that the accumulated total of U.S. assets held by foreigners began (in 1985) to exceed the total value of foreign assets held by the United States. That is how the United States became a debtor nation.

The United States went from being the world's largest creditor nation to the largest debtor nation in just five years (figure 2–4). This, in itself, is not a crisis situation, but it has some significant long-run implications. Certainly at the least it signals the erosion of U.S. dominance of the international economy, a dramatic change in the world role of the U.S. dollar's key currency status and the privileges that go with it, and a shift in the balance of economic power toward Japan and Western Europe, especially Japan, which became the world's

$ Billions

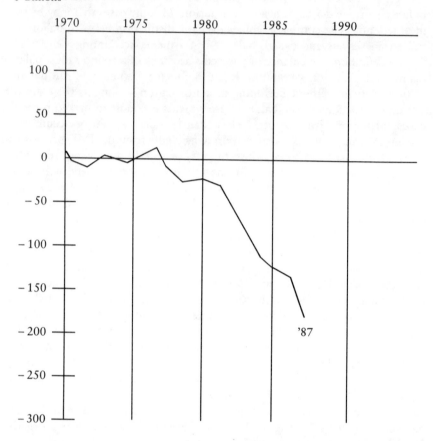

Source: *Economic Report of the President, 1988* (Washington, D.C.: Government Printing Office, 1988).

Figure 2–3. U.S. Merchandise Trade Balance, 1970–1987

largest creditor nation in 1986 (table 2–1). This unprecedented situation has a number of serious implications for the U.S. economy and for the rest of the world.

The federal debt, which we used to think was not a big problem because "we owed it to ourselves," is now increasingly being bought by foreigners. In 1976 foreign interests held only $70 billion of U.S. government securities, but by 1986 they owned $240 billion—a 350 percent increase in just ten years. Interest payments, which, it is important to emphasize, flow out of the country,

$ Billions

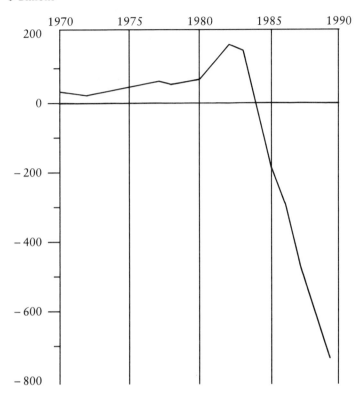

Source: U.S. Department of Commerce, *Survey of Current Business*, Vol. 68, No. 6, June 1988.

Figure 2–4. U.S. Net External Assets, 1970–1989

now amount to some $20 billion annually. In 1986 Japanese investors purchased around 35 percent of new long-term Treasury issues. If that trend continues, by 1996 foreign interests will own around $1 trillion of U.S. governmental obligations, and interest payments will be $100 billion (table 2–2).

Foreign investment involves more than just government securities; it involves direct purchases of U.S. corporations and real estate. Exact data on the extent of such investments are not available, but rough estimates are that foreign interests held $1.3 trillion in U.S. assets in 1987 and that over $200 billion of that was direct investment.[3] The list of well-known U.S. corporations now controlled by foreign interests is long—and getting longer. Economics columnist Ernest Conine has pointed out:

Table 2–1
Japan's Growing Role as a Creditor Nation
(billions)

	Net Overseas Investment	
	Japan	United States
1980	$ 11.5	$ 106.3
1981	10.9	141.1
1982	24.7	137.0
1983	37.3	89.6
1984	74.3	3.6
1985	129.8	– 111.9
1986	180.4	– 263.6

Source: U.S. Department of Commerce, *Survey of Current Business* Vol. 68, No. 6, June 1988.

If you were to require every foreign-owned enterprise to fly the national flag of its owners for a day, the result would surprise most Americans. Carnation Co. is Swiss. Doubleday, RCA Records, Celanese and General Tire are all German. Zale Corp., the giant jewelry retailer, is Canadian. Purina Mills, Smith and Wesson, and J. Walter Thompson advertising are British.

Because the Japanese were late starters, their investments are not much more than one-tenth as large as those of the Europeans. But the Japanese are coming on strong. Direct Japanese investment in the U.S. has more than tripled, to more than $25 billion, in just five years. Already Japanese banks have the largest foreign presence in the United States; they are especially strong in California.

Table 2–2
Japanese Foreign Assets in the United States, 1980–1987
(millions)

	Net Purchases[a]		Direct Investment
	Stocks	Bonds	
1980	$ 344	$ 4,285	$ 4,699
1981	240	5,808	8,932
1982	151	6,066	7,703
1983	658	12,507	8,145
1984	51	26,773	10,156
1985	995	53,517	12,217
1986	7,048	98,024	22,320
1987	10,019	48,497	7,461

Source: U.S. Department of Commerce, *Survey of Current Business*, Vol. 68, No. 6, June 1988.
Note: 1987 figures are for periods ended June 30. Stocks and bonds are based on calendar years; direct investment is based on fiscal years ended March 31.
[a]Excludes transactions of non-Japanese securities through Japanese market.

The Japanese also are plunging into the commercial real-estate market. Their holdings include the ARCO Plaza and Chase Plaza in Los Angeles, Essex House, and Exxon Building and Capital Cities–ABC headquarters in New York, plus major structures in Boston, Washington, San Francisco, Honolulu and other cities.

About 435 U.S. manufacturers in such disparate fields as auto assembly, chemicals, electronics, auto parts, textile equipment and steel products are owned wholly or partly by the Japanese.

In some sectors of the U.S. economy, foreign ownership has reached major proportions. Four of the top 10 chemical companies and more than half the cement industry are foreign-owned.[4]

It is often argued that such investments create jobs for Americans and stimulate the U.S. economy. That is true, but unless the profits from direct investments are reinvested in the United States (forever), they eventually flow abroad and exacerbate the already serious current account deficit. In the future, the situation is likely to worsen. Consider this possible scenario. In 1987 the balance-of-trade deficit was $171 billion, and the current account deficit (which includes trade and net investment flows) was $160 billion. If foreign investment increases at its present rate, the total current account deficit could easily exceed $1 trillion by the mid-1990s. Unless this is offset by capital inflows that exceed the (compounding) profit and interest outflows, the U.S. economy could well be brought to its knees as increasing percentages of its productive capacity are diverted abroad to service its foreign debt.

The net result is that because of the key role of the dollar as the international currency and the general strength of the U.S. economy, the United States has been able to run record-high levels of debt and enjoy the benefits of cheap imports through the 1980s. All of this is possible because it is being financed by foreign interests. But this situation cannot continue forever unless the United States is willing to sell its economy to the rest of the world.

Under the most favorable circumstances, the economies of the United States, Japan, and Western Europe will become melded into one giant supernational economy. A much less favorable scenario is that the U.S. economy will slip into a period of recession, or inflation, and foreign investors will lose faith in it and stop providing the capital—in essence, the loans—now required to service the U.S. federal deficit and the trade deficit and make the current fragile international financial system function. If that happens, the dollar could well collapse; imports would become prohibitively expensive, and this would put extreme inflationary pressures on the U.S. economy. To counter that and provide incentive for foreign investors to continue financing U.S. domestic deficits, interest rates would have to be pushed sky-high, pushing the economy into a recession. With U.S. markets shrinking, the rest of the world would also be pushed into a recession that could easily spiral into a full-fledged depression. The dollar would become "Monopoly money," and it would be the end of the era of privilege for Americans.

The ironic situation that the United States is rapidly moving into is similar but not exactly analogous to the even more serious and rapidly deteriorating debt crisis of the Third World. It is different in the sense that most of the U.S. external debt is privately held, whereas most of the Third World debt is governmental; and also the U.S. economy is much larger and stronger than any of the Third World countries—or all of them combined. In percentage terms the numbers are much less dramatic. But it is similar in the sense that sooner or later the United States will have to pay the price of debt and prolifigate spending habits by transferring resources out of the country and accepting a lower standing of living in return. That is exactly what is happening in the Third World now but for a different set of equally ironic reasons.

Third World Debt Crisis

The Third World debt crisis evolved in large part out of an unexpected and certainly unplanned quirk of fate. The Arab oil embargo of 1973 and the subsequent strengthening of the OPEC oil cartel resulted in a dramatic increase in oil prices and one of the largest transfers of wealth in history. Billions of dollars went to the Middle East from the oil import–dependent industrialized countries. They, in turn, redeposited the money in Western banks, which in turn loaned it to the capital-poor developing countries. At the time the process seemed to make sense to most analysts. Petrodollar recycling, as it was called, transferred funds to the place where they were most needed: the Third World.

It is worth reemphasizing that the rationale behind any country's borrowing from abroad—especially an underdeveloped country—is that if the funds are used productively by being invested in export-expanding sectors of the economy, overall welfare will be increased at the same time that the capacity to repay the loans is developed. On those assumptions, and the now-dubious assumption that governments do not go bankrupt, the international money center banks zealously facilitated the buildup of Third World debt. Third World foreign debt grew from $100 billion in 1973 to nearly $1 trillion in 1986 (figure 2–5).

But as early as 1982 it was becoming increasingly clear that a crisis of unprecedented proportions was brewing. High interest rates in the United States raised the cost of servicing the debt; the U.S. recession of the early 1980s reduced U.S. imports of Third World products, and world commodity prices fell. All this added up to the near-default by Mexico in 1982. The collapse of oil prices in 1986 pushed the oil-exporting Third World countries to the brink of collapse, and it was clear that the final link in the petrodollar cycle had been broken: the banks were not going to be repaid.

$ Billions

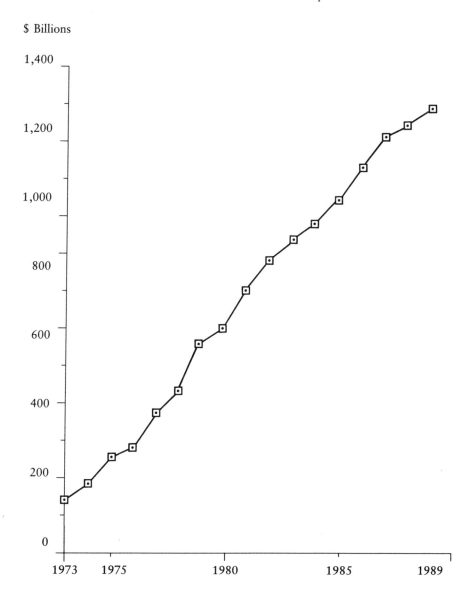

Source: World Bank, *World Bank Debt Tables: External Debt of Developing Countries* (Washington, D.C.: World Bank, 1987–88).

Figure 2–5. Third World Debt, 1973–1989

In the case of developing countries, the idea behind foreign borrowing and foreign investment is that a net flow of funds from the industrialized to the developing countries will be engendered by the lending process. If this does not happen, clearly it is ludicrous for any developing country to be borrowing for development purposes. Yet that is exactly what happened. The reasons are complicated and, ironically, built into the lending process.

The fundamental problem is that the mechanics of the lending process demonstrate that any situation that involves a regular annual amount of borrowing and a conventional repayment schedule will soon lead to a situation where the debt servicing (the interest and the amortization) will exceed the annual amount of new loans. This process will soon lead to a reverse capital flow (a flow of capital from the capital-poor to the capital-rich nations), which is the opposite of what one would presume was the desired effect.

This process is shown in figure 2–6, which presents a hypothetical example. Assume that each year a country obtains a new foreign loan of $1,000 to be repaid in equal installments over twenty years with 10 percent interest on the outstanding balance. The net result is a downward trend of net proceeds (the amount left over after paying the accumulated debt service, which gets larger and larger—due to paying interest on interest—making net proceeds get smaller and smaller). By the eighth year, the borrowing of an additional $1,000 is insufficient to meet the obligations on the past debt, so a reverse flow of funds back to the lending country begins unless the rate of new borrowing is increased.

Any time a country borrows a constant amount of new funds each year to be repaid at a given rate of interest, the return flow of interest and principal amortization will eventually exceed the inflow of new loans, creating a reverse flow of funds to the creditor country, quite the opposite of what is supposed to happen. How long this takes depends on how high the rate of interest is, but in the case of Latin America, for one example, it was about twenty years.

The net inflow of loan funds to the developing countries was increasing until 1981, when it started to decrease (figure 2–7). By 1983 the reverse flow had begun; the creditor countries were receiving more than they were lending. The "development" loan process was causing a net drain of capital from the debtor countries.

The key factor in determining the viability of such a loan-based development strategy is the percentage of total export revenues that a country must commit to debt servicing. If export earnings are increasing faster than the flow of debt service, then—by this measure at least—the program is viable. In this context a look at the data is revealing.

Debt service as a percentage of export revenues was 16 percent in 1980 but grew to almost 23 percent by 1984 (table 2–3). This is in a period where

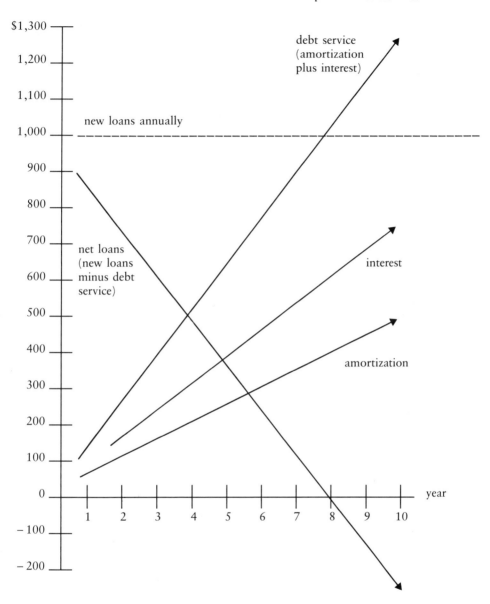

Source: *Monthly Review* (April 1985).
Note: Net capital flow if $1,000 is borrowed each year at 10 percent interest for twenty years.

Figure 2–6. The Debt Trap

U.S. $ Billions

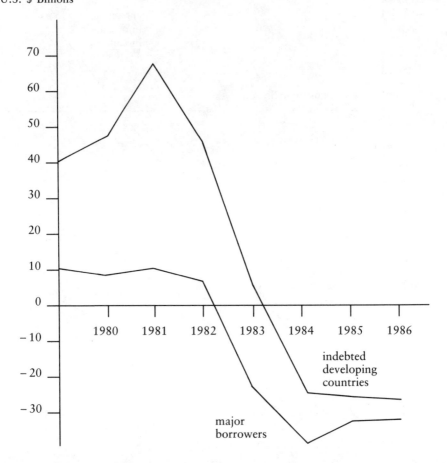

Source: Harold Lever and Christopher Huhne, *Debt and Danger: The World Financial Crisis* (New York: Atlantic Monthly Press, 1986).

Figure 2–7. The Resource Transfer, 1979–1986

Third World exports have been increasing—in an effort to service the debt—while imports have been pared to the lowest possible level. This has had two effects, both of which are becoming increasingly serious and illustrate the senselessness of the process.

Exports and Imports: A Two-Way Street
A country can service increasing debt obligations by increasing its exports. In an era of falling commodity prices and, especially, declining oil prices, this

Table 2–3
Debt and Financial Flows in Developing Countries, 1980–1987
(U.S. billions)

	1981	1982	1983	1984	1985	1986ᵃ	1987ᵃ
Debt disbursed and outstanding	$498.0	$556.9	$639.4	$713.8	$783.6	$870.7	$930.5
Disbursements	124.3	116.6	99.1	92.3	88.7	85.7	90.0
(from private creditors)	91.4	84.2	66.5	58.6	57.3	47.5	49.0
Debt service	89.1	98.7	92.1	99.7	109.5	116.4	119.0
Principal repayments	47.5	49.7	44.7	46.8	54.8	60.8	64.0
Interest	41.7	48.9	47.2	52.8	54.7	55.6	55.0
Net transfers	35.2	17.8	7.1	− 7.3	− 20.8	− 30.7	− 29.0

Source: World Bank, *World Debt Tables*, I (Washington, D.C.: World Bank, 1988).
Note: The 109 countries reporting under the Debtor Reporting System (DRS). Data for Poland are included only from 1984 onward.
ᵃPreliminary for 1986; estimated for 1987.

has not generally been a feasible strategy. Third World exports to the industrialized nations did increase during the 1980s, bringing about some improvement in developing countries' current account situation (table 2–4), but most of the improvement—if that is what it can be called—came not from increases in exports but from decreases in imports. The net effect is that badly needed replacement parts, equipment, and new technology have not been available in most Third World countries, so their economic growth has ground to a halt, if not become negative. This, coupled with high rates of population growth, has meant that already low standards of living in most of the debtor countries have declined precipitously. The standard of living in Mexico, to take just one example, has fallen to where it was in 1967, causing much human suffering, not to mention political unrest.

The other side of that coin is even more ironic. Third World imports are the exports of the industrialized world (table 2–5). In the United States, the loss of exports to Latin America alone accounted in 1987 for around 25 percent of the U.S. trade deficit. That translated into the loss of around 1 million export-related jobs, or about 13 percent of the U.S. unemployment rate. So, simply to perpetuate the myth that the international banking system is functioning, both the industrialized world and the Third World are paying a very high price.

The Banks and U.S. Government Policy

In the early years of the crisis—from 1980 until 1986—the policy of the U.S. money center banks was to continue lending more and more money to the debtor countries in order to allow them to service at least the interest on what

Table 2–4
Third World Debtor Countries Trade Balance, 1975–1986
(U.S. millions)

Year	Exports	Imports	Trade Balance
1975	$171,757	$224,343	−$52,586
1980	447,196	550,108	−102,912
1981	470,415	602,047	−131,632
1982	440,839	569,760	−128,921
1983	434,393	521,815	−87,422
1984	471,571	533,843	−62,272
1985	463,018	540,613	−77,595
1986	450,235	529,215	−78,980

Source: World Bank, *World Debt Tables*, I (Washington, D.C.: World Bank, 1988).

they already owed. This, as all of the involved parties know, merely serves to compound and perpetuate a clearly unworkable situation. The official U.S. government policy, which takes the form of the Baker plan, is that both private bank and governmental loans should be continued on the condition that the debtor countries restructure their economies. This, in essence, means privatizing inefficient state-controlled industries and letting market forces operate more freely, under the auspices of an IMF-approved austerity plan. IMF austerity plans typically involve cutting back inflation by keeping a tight rein on the money supply, reducing government expenditures, and instituting wage controls—all of which add up to a reduction in the standard of living.

Some of the larger debtor countries, such as Mexico and Argentina, agreed to cooperate with the IMF and the commercial banks, and new loan packages were arranged for them in 1986 and 1987, adding billions to their overall debt but temporarily forestalling a crisis. Others, notably Brazil and Peru, have balked at instituting austerity measures and have declared moratoriums or similar measures on even interest payments on their debts.

Table 2–5
Highly Indebted Countries, GDP, Exports, and Imports, 1980–1987
(% real increase or decrease)

Year	GDP	Exports	Imports
1980	5.7	3.8	10.9
1981	0.4	−1.1	6.1
1982	−0.6	−5.0	−14.3
1983	−2.9	1.7	−20.2
1984	2.3	12.3	−2.4
1985	2.9	−0.5	0.1
1986	2.9	−2.7	−0.7
1987	2.4	1.5	−0.9

Source: World Bank, *World Debt Tables*, I (Washington, D.C.: World Bank, 1988).

Brazil's recalcitrance prompted a major reassessment of the entire Third World debt problem by the commercial banks. Many of the U.S. money center banks were in 1986 exposed in amounts far exceeding their capitalization (table 2–6).[5] Banks can carry such loans on their books as performing so long as interest payments are not more than ninety days in arrears. After that loans must be transferred to a cash basis and assets—or what is called assets—reduced accordingly. Faced with such a prospect and the possibility of a domino-like series of defaults in Latin America, Citicorp, the largest U.S. bank and the holder of almost $16 billion in Third World loans, unilaterally called Brazil's bluff and increased its reserves against loan losses by some $3 billion. In the process it took an accounting loss of $2.5 billion in the second quarter of 1987—the largest in U.S. banking history. The other large banks had no choice but to follow suit, and by the summer of 1987 loan-loss reserves of the ten largest U.S. banks had been increased by $11 billion.

This unexpected action was the first time that the major banks had publicly acknowledged that the Third World debt situation was an illusory game being played with mirrors, and it represents an important turning point in the history of the debt crisis.

Table 2–6
Bank Loan Exposure to Developing Nations, 1986
(U.S. millions)

Bank	Assets	Total Third World Loans	Loans as a Percentage of Capital
Bank of New York	$ 20,709	$ 505	40
BankAmerica	104,189	6,681	108
Bankers Trust	53,743	2,128	66
Chase Manhattan	94,766	6,700	125
Chemical	60,564	4,367	115
Citicorp	196,124	14,700	137
Continental Illinois	32,809	1,560	63
First Chicago	39,148	1,674	57
First Interstate	55,422	2,267	69
First Pennsylvania	5,888	537	104
Irving	24,233	1,416	111
J.P. Morgan	76,039	3,939	65
Manufacturers Hanover	74,397	7,505	157
Marine Midland	24,790	1,474	90
Mellon	33,406	898	45
Republic Bank of New York	16,814	570	34
Security Pacific	62,606	1,251	34
Wells Fargo	44,577	1,534	50

Source: Bear Stearns, *The Wall Street Journal*, July 14, 1987.
Note: Money center banks whose loans to developing nations exceeded 33 percent of their capital—that is, equity plus reserves for losses on loans—at the end of 1986.

The get-tough stance by the banks signaled the debtor countries that timely payments would have to be made, or they would face the prospect of being cut out of badly needed trade credits. The banks, by increasing their reserves against losses, were saying that they were ready to "take the hit" if necessary. The markets, knowing that Third World debt was already selling at around 55 percent of stated value, generally perceived this move as prudent banking, and indeed the banks' stock value increased in spite of huge losses.

But the banks' get-tough attitude could easily become the straw that breaks the camel's back. The key point here is that the annual flow of new loans must equal or exceed the return flow of debt service. Otherwise the debtor country simply slides backward, as has been happening since 1982. If the flow of new loans stops altogether or is curtailed, the old loans, with debt servicing obligations, are still there. Under such circumstances, any underdeveloped debtor economy will quickly collapse under the weight of payment obligations with no corresponding cash inflow.

Before the banks increased their loan-loss reserves, new loans to the fifteen debtor countries had fallen by $2.8 billion, and governmental and international agency loans dropped to $6.6 billion in 1986, compared to an average of $13.8 billion in 1983 and 1984. Since there is no way that any commercial bank can make a profit by granting dubious, risky new loans while at the same increasing its loan-loss reserves, it is highly unlikely that the flow of new funds to the underdeveloped debtor countries will continue at anywhere near the levels of the early 1980s.

As the debtor countries begin to perceive that new funds are not likely to be forthcoming and as political pressures to get off the debt treadmill mount, the likelihood of a unilateral default is becoming ever greater. If one major debtor country should repudiate its foreign debt, the others might follow. While the banks' recent loan-loss reserve increases would help soften the blow, the international financial system could not withstand such a shock without a major bail-out from the governments of the industrialized countries.

The effects of a default on the U.S. economy would be devastating. No one has put it more eloquently than former secretary of treasury and White House chief of staff Donald Regan, who in testimony before a congressional committee said:

> The American citizen has the right to ask why he or his government need to be concerned with debt problems abroad. With high unemployment at home, why should we be assisting other countries, rather than, say, reducing taxes or increasing spending domestically? Why should he care what happens to the international financial system?
>
> One way to look at this question is to ask what the implications are for workers in Providence, Pascoag, or Woonsocket if foreign borrowers do not receive sufficient assistance to adjust in an orderly way. What if they are late in making interest payments to banks or can't pay principal, and loans become nonperforming or are written off as a loss?

If interest payments are more than ninety days late, the banks stop accruing them on their books; they suffer reduced profits and bear the costs of continued funding of the loan. Provisions may have to be made for loss, and as loans are actually written off, the capital of the bank is reduced.

This in turn reduces the banks' capital asset ratio, which forces banks to curtail lending to individual borrowers and lowers the overall total they can lend. The reduction in the amounts banks can lend will impact on the economy. So will the banks' reduced ability to make investments, which in everyday language includes the purchase of municipal bonds which help to finance the operations of the communities where individual Americans work and live. Reduced ability to lend could also raise interest rates.

I want to make very clear, Mr. Chairman, that we are not talking here just about the big money-center banks and the multinational corporations. Well over 1,500 U.S. banks, or more than 10 percent of the total number of U.S. banks, have loaned money to Latin America alone. They range in size from over $100 billion in assets to about $100 million. Those banks are located in virtually every state, in virtually every Congressional district, and in virtually every community of any size in the country. Those loans, among other things, financed exports, exports that resulted in jobs, housing and investment being maintained or created throughout the United States.

If the foreign borrowers are not able to service those loans, not only will U.S. banks not be able to continue lending abroad, they will have to severely curtail their lending in the United States. Let me illustrate this point as graphically as I can. A sound, well-run U.S. bank of $10 billion in assets—not all that large today—might have capital of $600 million. It is required by the regulators to maintain the ratio of at least $6 in capital to every $100 in assets. What happens if 10 percent, or $60 million of its capital, is eroded through foreign loan losses? It must contract its lending by $1 billion. Now realistically, the regulators will not force it to contract immediately, but they will force it to restrict its growth until its capital can be rebuilt.

The new result in either event is 11 billion in loans that can't be made in that community—20,000 home mortgages at $50,000 each that can't be financed, or 10,000 lines of credit to local businesses at $100,000 each that can't be extended.

And of course, this reduction in lending will have negative effects of financing of exports, imports, domestic investment, and production in individual cities and states around the United States, be it in shipping, tourist facilities, farming, or manufacturing. The impact will not only be on the banks—it will negatively affect the individual as well as the economic system as a whole. Higher unemployment and a reduction in economic activity, with all they entail for city, state, and federal budgets, would be a further result. None of this is in the interest of the U.S. citizen.[6]

The United States has woven itself a complex, spider-like web in which it has now become entangled. The preeminence of the dollar as the international key currency and the privileges that went with it are now history. The unplanned, and certainly unexpected, events of the past two decades are inextricably intertwined (figure 2–8). The buildup of public and private debt in the United States

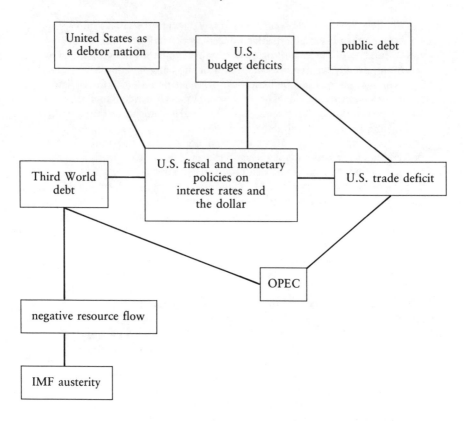

Figure 2–8. The Triple Debt Crisis

makes it a prisoner of the international economy, dependent on the goodwill of the new creditor nations, most notably Japan. Moreover, the apparent inability of U.S. industry to compete internationally and the continuing balance-of-trade deficits that do not respond to even massive dollar devaluations seem to indicate that a solution is not on the horizon. The interrelated Third World debt crisis, which exacerbates the trade crisis and shows the vulnerability of the U.S. banking system to external shocks, has every indication of getting worse.

A triple debt crisis has evolved. U.S. internal debt, U.S. external debt, and the Third World debt cannot be allowed to escalate much further, or we can expect a dramatic shift in the balance of economic power. Realistic new policies are called for. The international financial system must be restructured to reflect the realities of the modern world. If it is not, we can expect a drastic reduction in standards of living, both in the United States and throughout the world.

This is not to say that there is a shortage of ideas about how to solve the problem, just that none will work unless they encompass the longer-run structural contradictions of the United States—once the dominant economic power in the world, able to make its own rules—now being reduced to the status of a debt-ridden country. There are solutions, but they will require sacrifices. Above all it is becoming obvious that the world economy cannot continue to function as it has in the past. Change will come. Whether it is planned and orderly, or unplanned and chaotic, is the question yet to be resolved.

3
Reconstructing the International Financial System

In order for international trade to function, there has to be a system upon which every participant agrees to make international exchange payments possible. So long as everyone agrees that something is universally acceptable and convertible into local currency, trade will take place, to everyone's benefit. That "something" must perform all of the traditional functions of money in any economy; it must be a medium of exchange for transactions, a store of value for reserves, and a unit of account, so people, businesses, and nations can keep track of what is going on and plan accordingly.

Gold performed that function for many hundreds of years. But by the end of World War II, it was becoming obvious that gold was too cumbersome and limited in supply to perform its traditional role effectively. This was especially complicated by the fact that at that time the United States held most of the world's minted gold supply. Another option, supported by many of the participants in the Bretton Woods Conference, would have been to set up a world monetary authority with the power to issue a universally acceptable currency that could be used to settle international accounts. But such a system would have had all of the restrictions and limitations of the gold system, and the United States, in particular, opposed it. Another equally workable system is for the world to agree that one country's currency will be acceptable to all at an agreed-upon rate of exchange. Since the United States was the dominant economic power at the time, it was decided that the U.S. dollar would become the world's key international currency. This set the stage for an era of U.S. dominance of the world economy and for the present economic crisis and the eventual demise of U.S. hegemony.

At first the system seemed to work well. The United States agreed to peg the value of the dollar to a set amount of gold—$35 an ounce—and to redeem dollars held by foreign countries at that rate on demand. That meant, for all practical purposes, that the dollar was as "good as gold" universally acceptable for international transactions and suitable for foreign bank reserves. It also meant that the United States accepted responsibility for the smooth functioning of the international financial system, which, in essence, meant that it was agreeing to maintain the value of the dollar at a constant rate because no monetary system can function if its users do not know from day to day what the value of the key currency will be.

Also at the Bretton Woods Conference the IMF was established to monitor exchange rates within a narrow band (plus or minus 1 percent) against the U.S. dollar. Therefore a system of international economic discipline was instituted that had all the trappings of the gold standard. If a country was running a balance-of-payments deficit, thereby causing a drop in the demand for its currency and a consequent drop in its value, it had no option but to institute appropriate domestic economic policies to correct the situation. This meant slowing down its rate of inflation at the cost of slower growth and higher unemployment or devaluing its currency, which required permission of the U.S.-controlled IMF.

Every country in the Western world was therefore subjected to the discipline of the international financial system except the United States, which could do whatever it wanted. So long as there was a strong demand for dollars (to pay for much-needed U.S. exports) and the United States had the gold to back them up, the system functioned smoothly for, in fact, about fifteen years. But by the 1960s, as the war-torn economies of Western Europe and Japan began to recover (due in large part to reconstruction loans from the United States) and became major exporters in their own right, the situation began to change. The U.S. balance-of-payments surplus dwindled while Japan and Western Europe, now operating with newer, more productive plants and equipment, began to run large surpluses, selling more to the United States than they were buying and accumulating large dollar balances in the process.

The Collapse of Bretton Woods

By 1971 it had become obvious that the United States no longer had the wherewithal to back the dollar. Dollar holdings abroad exceeded $70 billion, while the U.S. gold supply dwindled to around $10 billion. It was clear that the world's banker no longer had the reserves to make good on its claim that the dollar was as good as gold. In 1971 President Nixon cut the link between gold and the dollar. In December of that year the financial ministers of the Western world met in Washington and reluctantly agreed (the Smithsonian Agreement) that the world was now on a dollar system with none of the traditional link to gold and no disciplinary restraints on exchange rate fluctuations.

The international financial system was now left to the vicissitudes of the forces of the free market. The new system was a free-flexible-floating exchange rate system, but the U.S. dollar was still the world's key international currency. Put differently, the world economy became dependent on the U.S. economy for stability, and the discipline of the gold standard and the Bretton Woods agreements had become history. The problem now was for the United States to discipline itself.

So long as the U.S. economy remained strong and stable, there was no particular problem associated with this dramatic change in the rules of how international trade was to be conducted. If dollars are relatively constant in value and in demand, they can function as a medium of international exchange as well as anything else. But while dollars continued to be in demand, their value did not remain constant. Several events that were largely unanticipated and certainly unexpected occurred to change that.

Inflation Shocks

On the heels of the Smithsonian Agreement, the OPEC oil embargo and the subsequent fourfold increase in the price of oil by 1973 sent an inflationary shock throughout the U.S. economy. Under such conditions, one would normally expect the exchange rate of the dollar to fall as U.S. exports become more expensive, but the OPEC countries demanded that payments for oil be made in U.S. dollars, thereby increasing the demand for the dollar worldwide. At the same time, the recycling of petrodollars to the Third World increased demand for U.S. exports. The dollar became stronger even in the face of higher rates of inflation in the United States. By the time inflation rates peaked in the United States at over 10 percent in 1982, the dollar was still becoming stronger until it peaked in the fall of 1985 (figure 3–1).

As a result of this, and many other factors that we shall explore in the following chapter, the U.S. trade balance began to decline precipitously—from a deficit of $36 billion in 1982 to a $171 billion deficit in 1987. If a country is going to serve as the world's banker, it has to maintain some stability in its international accounts. If the United States runs a trade surplus, then as foreigners scramble for dollars to buy U.S. products, dollars are taken out of the world economy and international liquidity is reduced, among other things. But if the owner of the world's anchor linchpin currency runs a consistent trade deficit, then something else has to occur in the overall flow of international transactions to cover, or pay for, the deficit; otherwise the value of the currency will fall. Interestingly these offsetting transactions did occur as other countries continued to pour the dollars earned (from exports to the United States) back into the United States as foreign investment, which is another way of saying the United States borrowed the money to finance its trade deficit. This has caused the United States to move, in just a few years, from being the world's largest creditor nation to being the world's largest debtor and has precipitated a crisis in the international financial system of unprecedented and seeming unsolvable proportions.

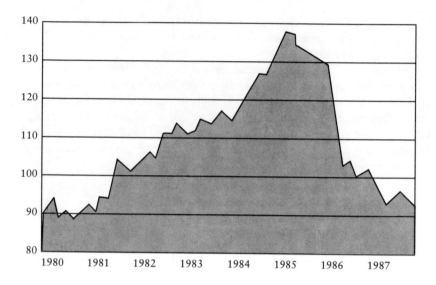

Source: *Economic Report of the President, 1988* (Washington, D.C.: Government Printing Office, 1988).

Note: 1980–1982 = 100.

Figure 3–1. Index of the Dollar's Value against Fifteen Industrial Country Currencies

Ironically, although the United States is the largest debtor nation, it remains one of the largest creditors in the sense that it holds debts of the Third World—now generally acknowledged to be unrepayable. For the pillar of the world economy to be debtor and a creditor at the same time is clearly untenable over anybody's definition of long run. Attempts to rectify the situation by devaluating the dollar by some 50 percent between 1985 and 1988 have failed; the U.S. trade deficit has continued at record-high levels. The dollar, the world's key currency, is being propped up by ad hoc intervention in the exchange markets. Clearly the United States has lost control of its own economy—as debt is replaced by new debt at a compound rate—and most certainly it has lost control of the international economy.

Other factors, external to and clearly outside U.S. control, have made it clear to most analysts that the world has changed in ways that no one would have expected at the time of the first Bretton Woods Conference. Most important, Japan has become the world's largest creditor nation, West Germany and much of the rest of Western Europe are not far behind, and gaining on them are the NICs of the Pacific rim. This shift in the balance of economic power, which has occurred in only one decade, is unprecedented. All the rules, the traditions, and the structure of the dollar-based system are coming into question, leading an increasing number of observers to call for a new Bretton Woods conference: a complete restructuring of the international financial system more in line with the reality of the modern world.

A New Bretton Woods?

There is general agreement that any restructuring of the international financial system must address the problem of more equitable flows of trade and capital. This means, in essence, that the Third World debt problem must be addressed and resolved. Any system that does not resolve this problem will simply prolong and exacerbate the current crisis. There is less agreement, however, on how to go about it.

The Case Against

There are also those who argue that a new system is unnecessary because the current system already has mechanisms to correct the imbalance. The IMF, some argue, could initiate the necessary discussions and implement appropriate policies. But the IMF already holds annual conferences, and little seems to be accomplished. Indeed, many argue, the conservative policies of the IMF, which attempt to correct exchange rate distortions through "conditional" loans, have been one of the primary causes of the problem.

Others argue that the current problems could easily be resolved if the United States would put in place appropriate monetary and fiscal policies to end inflation and lower interest rates. But that has already happened over the past several years, and the overall situation has continued to worsen.

A related argument is that a restructuring of the international financial system is almost certain to be opposed by any U.S. administration, so even thinking about it is a waste of time. Nevertheless, the crisis has reached such proportions and the trends are so troubling that soon there will be no choice. The question is whether the process will be planned and orderly or forced and chaotic. Morris Miller, former executive director of the World Bank, has made an insightful analysis of the problem:

> It matters whether the movement toward a new Bretton Woods is made by design or forced by events. The preferred method is to be guided by forethought and design, but even the second-best route to the destination may suffice—if we don't fall off the figurative cliff in the meantime. Once the current debt crisis is seen as an integral part of a deep-seated transformation of the global economic and financial system, the door is open to considering policy approaches that have the breadth and depth commensurate to the problem.[1]

There is a growing recognition that a turning point requiring a series of hard choices is imminent. There is, however, less recognition that the profound changes wrought over the past four decades are of a structural nature in terms of how trade and finance are handled and the size and direction of these flows, and the ability of the United States to take on the type of leadership responsibilities that were assumed at Bretton Woods and the necessity of sharing such leadership with Japan and other nations.

The Case For

Under such conditions it is not surprising that, in the light of the present instability of the international financial system, there are increasing calls for a new system based on something more stable than the U.S. dollar, which is now out of control both literally and figuratively. Even such staid observers of the international scene as former secretary of state Henry Kissinger have taken up the cause:

> The biggest politico-economic challenge to statesmen is to integrate national policies into a global perspective, to resolve the discordance between the international economy and the political system based on the nation state. . . . The spirit that produced Bretton Woods reflected the realization that in the long run the national welfare can only be safeguarded within the framework of the general welfare. . . . In [today's] circumstances the international economic system operates—if at all—as crisis management. The risk is, of course, that some day crisis management may be inadequate. The world will then face a disaster its lack of foresight has made inevitable. . . . My major point is that the world needs new arrangements.[2]

Put in this context, the rationale for international monetary reform seems overwhelming because no system of policy coordination exists to replace the declining U.S. leadership role; there is no early warning system designed to signal impending crisis and no adequate response mechanism to cope with crises when they do occur; and there is no control mechanism over the mobility of capital. Foreign exchange transactions conducted instantaneously by computer links now amount to more than $200 billion a day.[3]

The agenda for a new Bretton Woods is a long one, and the issues are pressing to the point of urgency. As the stock market crash on October 19, 1987—"Black Monday"—dramatically demonstrated, the financial system cannot function efficiently in such a volatile climate.

Agenda for a New Bretton Woods

Those who favor a new Bretton Woods conference argue that it should not be held in a climate of panic, should not be held without considerable prior preparation, and should not attempt to map out a plan for what might be done in the future. Rather, they suggest, it must address the fundamental structural imbalances that are disrupting the present outmoded system.

In *Toward World Prosperity*, a penetrating book on the topic, Irving Friedman has suggested six basic issues that must be included in a new Bretton Woods conference if it is to be successful.

First, a new financial system must be developed that will provide the framework for world prosperity, sustained growth, and structural change. Such a system must above all protect the developing countries from the continuing and worsening levels of high unemployment, low growth rates, and inadequate rates of saving.

Second, a system of exchange rates must be established that is realistic, equitable, and stable. Many of the present problems have come from the continual roller coaster–like movements of the dollar from strong to weak, weak to strong, a process that has disrupted the smooth functioning of the system, helped no one, and generated unnecessary instability and uncertainty.

Third, the process of international capital movements must be reexamined. Capital is supposed to move from the more industrialized world to the underdeveloped countries. Instead, the opposite has occurred. If the system is to regain stability, this must be corrected. Is it feasible, Friedman asks, for a code of international behavior in this area to be established? If so, who would administer it?

Fourth, something has to be done to stop persistent worldwide inflation, which has reached epidemic proportions in the underdeveloped countries and is a persistent problem in the industrialized world as well. No one knows how to stop inflation without at the same time slowing economic growth and increasing unemployment, a bitter pill that few nations are willing to swallow. Is it feasible, he asks, that exchange rate adjustments could be tied to inflation rates in a more formal manner, perhaps administered by the IMF?

Fifth, Friedman asks:

> Do the existing governmental rules and practices serve world business, which has become interdependent and integrated to a degree that represents a quantum change from the past? . . .
>
> Interdependence and global integration have created a world in which nations and their businesses have lost their freedom of action, however, reluctantly and angrily. The linkages of world markets . . . mean new definitions of what is national, what is meant by national interest, and what is meant by unfair national competitive practices.

Finally, he asks, "Is the international financial system suited to a world that has become very different because of the miracles of modern technology?"[4]

The Major Question: Policy Coordination

Any restructuring of the international financial system must be considered in the context of overall policy coordination between the major industrial powers and between them and the less developed countries, which include some 4 billion people, 80 percent of the world's population. The present system gives only lip-service to policy coordination—as was evident at the Venice Summit—while each of the industrial powers continues beggar-thy-neighbor policies of studied self-interest that do not have long-run viability.

In a sense there has been an international economic policy in place since 1980: a policy of no policy. The theoretical rationale of the Reagan administration has been that capitalism functions best when it is left alone. When it became clear in 1985 that laissez-faire economics did not always work to everyone's advantage, especially that of the United States, haphazard intervention in the exchange markets became the "policy" that pushed the dollar down by some 50 percent against the currencies of the major U.S. trading partners. That move produced virtually no results; the U.S. trade deficit hovered at levels over $150 billion two years after the intervention. And *policy coordination,* which is simply another way of saying "international economic planning," became the buzz-word in Washington and in the financial press.

For international policy coordination to have any long-run effect, three key questions have to be addressed. First, trade imbalances must be resolved or, at least, financed in an orderly manner. Second, exchange rates must be stabilized and anchored to something that provides stability, as well as coordinated flexibility. Third, capital flows must be redirected to where they produce growth rather than engender long-run stagnation. In addition, and directly related to the problem of capital flows, the Third World debt crisis must be resolved. Until that happens, talk of a new Bretton Woods conference and policy coordination will ring as hollow as the rhetoric of laissez-faire.

Coordination and Trade

The issues that must be addressed at a new Bretton Woods conference fall into three major but interrelated categories: trade imbalance, a workable system of exchange rate adjustment, and capital flows (in the present reality, the Third World debt question). The latter two are subsets of the overall trade question.

So long as the United States continues to run record-high trade deficits and, essentially, exchange those deficits for recycled paper IOUs, the international financial system will continue to be dangerously fragile and the United States will pay the price, as will the Third World debtor countries. The problem could perhaps be resolved by increasing U.S. manufacturing productivity—through restoring the U.S. competitive position and/or devising some way to induce reluctant Japan and West Germany (and others) to stimulate their economies to the extent that they could absorb more U.S. exports—or by convincing U.S. consumers to reduce the level of consumption of imported products.

Although there are indications that U.S. productivity is improving, there is little evidence that the trade imbalance, which is also gradually improving, will reverse itself to the extent that it would make any real difference in the foreseeable future. A new Bretton Woods conference cannot dictate to American consumers, cannot tell U.S. industry to be more productive, and certainly cannot tell Japanese, European, South Korean, and Taiwanese manufacturers to stop trying to sell their products abroad. Therefore the burden falls on an agreement that will stabilize exchange rates at levels consistent with trade equilibrium and on one designed to normalize capital flows, at least to the extent that funds begin flowing from the industrialized world to the developing world instead of the reverse, as is happening now. There are many proposals to modify the exchange rate system and to rectify the Third World debt problem. Some are viable; some, in the current political climate, are not. Whether any kind of change in the exchange rate system would be sufficient to resolve the overall problem of imbalance and inequality in the international remains to be seen.

The Exchange Rate Problem

Since 1985 the Reagan administration has been consciously allowing the value of the dollar to decline in an effort to make U.S. exports more competitive and imports more expensive. This strategy has been somewhat less than successful. Although the dollar has declined as much as 40 percent against the yen and deutsche mark (figure 3–2), the U.S. merchandise trade deficit for 1987 was a record $171.2 billion. The dollar decline did generate a significant 20 percent increase in manufacturing exports; yet the U.S. appetite for the even more expensive imports continued unabated.

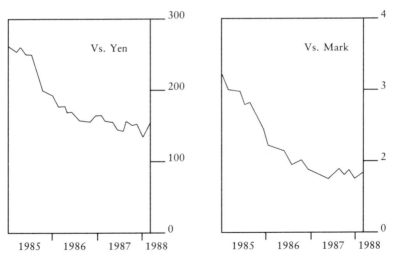

Source: *World Economic Outlook: A Survey by the Staff of the IMF*, Washington, D.C.: IMF, 1988.

Figure 3–2. Average Monthly Exchange Rates of the Dollar since March 1985

Several prominent economists, including former chairman of the Council of Economic Advisors Martin Feldstein, have suggested that the dollar should be allowed to fall further.[5] This position suggested that the bottom has not yet been reached. But the Reagan administration has been cautious about letting the dollar sink too low and too fast given the need to finance the federal deficit and maintain interest rates at levels high enough to keep attracting foreign money. So one of two things has happened: either there is something wrong with the economic theory guiding exchange rate policy, or there are structural factors at work in the economy thwarting exchange rate policy. It is clear that as Professor Paul Krugman, an international economist from MIT, has pointed out: "The U.S. trade balance has shown less turnaround than anyone's model predicted."[6] In theory, according to Robert Kuttner, "the decline of the dollar since 1985 should have resulted in a reversal of export and import prices. But instead much less of the yen and deutsche mark appreciation has been passed through to American consumers in the form of higher import prices than was expected. This explains the high level of imports and the continued high trade deficit. The trade-weighted dollar has declined 28.8 percent since 1985 while import prices have increased only 18.8 percent."[7]

Many economists have attempted to explain the lack of success of the U.S. exchange rate policy in terms of the J curve. J-curve theory argues that at first there will be a rise in the trade deficit after the dollar declines because consumers only slowly adjust to the higher-priced imports. After consumers adjust, a reduction in imports will occur as exports are expanding, and the trade deficit will begin to decline. This has not been the case. Although there have been some improvements in the U.S. trade deficit, the failure of the J-curve theory continues to be an enigma, and there is no simple explanation.

By the mid-1980s, foreign producers had successfully held down their export prices despite the enormous changes in currency values prompted by the U.S. devaluation of the dollar, so the relative prices of imports and domestic products did not change significantly. This limited the predicted benefits of a cheaper dollar. What appears to have happened is that foreign companies, especially Japanese firms, are more adept at pricing to the market, that is, adjusting to competitive conditions, than expected. U.S. firms seem to be less successful in adjusting pricing policies to market conditions changed by currency value shifts.

How do foreign companies manage to hold down export prices in the face of a declining dollar? Or, put differently, why are U.S. firms unable to price to the market? Harvard economist Jeffrey Sachs has argued and demonstrated that the focus on the dollar itself is allowing for a misdirected policy. He believes that the dollar strategy, which largely is based upon monetary policy (the manipulation of interest rates), is wrong because it does not address the reality of the U.S. budget deficits and the relationship of these deficits to the trade deficit. Sachs maintains that the low interest rates required to encourage the decline of the dollar also encourage consumer spending and demand for imports. In addition, the existence of budget deficits (in the vicinity of $160 billion a year) stimulates consumer demand for imports because discretionary income is larger than would be the case if taxes were increased or spending decreased in an attempt to reduce the budget deficits. Therefore both lower interest rates and budget deficits drive the seemingly insatiable demand for imports on the part of American consumers in spite of the falling dollar.[8]

There are, in addition, other factors behind the lack of success of the dollar devaluation strategy, which help explain why the prices of imported goods have not followed the appreciation of the yen and deutsche mark. Economist Robert Kuttner has identified five major explanations:

1. Most raw materials are priced in dollars. Therefore a 70 percent decline in the dollar also means a 70 percent decline in the cost of oil, iron ore, chemical feedstocks, and other commodities, substantially offsetting the effect of the higher exchange rate on the price of finished products.

2. All currencies have not appreciated against the dollar. Both American and Japanese producers have increasingly moved production to cheap-currency, low-wage countries like Korea, Taiwan, Singapore, China, and Mexico.

3. Capital costs are far lower in Japan and Germany than in the United States. This means that a Japanese firm can cut profit margins to hold the line on prices and still make acceptable returns.

4. Many foreign producers did not pass along the full savings to U.S. customers when the dollar was expensive, so they had a substantial cushion to absorb anticipated price increases as the dollar got cheaper.

5. A large share of imports today are marketed in the United States by American retailers or wholesalers, who often share the foreign producer's interest in holding down the price.[9]

These factors make it clear that the decline of the dollar will not automatically reduce the trade deficit. The present one-dimensional policy approach will result only in a decline in the standard of living of U.S. citizens as the cost of imports increases and inflation follows. The gradual resurgence in U.S. exports, while a positive factor, is tempered by the fact that continued export growth is held captive by the continued growth of other advanced industrial nations' export capacity and by the decrease in the demand for U.S. exports by developing nations because of their inability to maintain growth rates and export earnings sufficient to service their debt and at the same time buy more U.S. exports. A U.S. recession would exacerbate all of these issues.

To complicate this situation further, the global economy is suffering from excess capacity, especially for export-oriented goods like steel and automobiles. There is also the problem that many U.S. firms that successfully adapted to the new competitive environment of the 1980s now find themselves so lean that they are unable to increase output without higher costs or having to expand their capacity, so it is unlikely that they will be inclined to expand capacity rapidly in the short run to take advantage of what may be only a temporary increase in demand in the face of a potential global recession in 1989 or 1990. Another problem is that many firms fully dismantled their marketing networks when the dollar was strong and are unable to respond swiftly to the new, more competitive conditions. Finally the maze of regulations (peculiar to every nation in this interdependent global economy) makes doing business more difficult and time-consuming, thus slowing any rapaid response to changing currency swings. Faced with this set of realities and uncertainties, it is virtually impossible for firms to make decisions about whether to expand capacity at all or where to add it in the face of increasing global production.

It seems clear that a weaker dollar will not cure the trade deficit. Deborah Allen Oliver, president of Clarement Economics Institute, has argued that "the dollar's plunge against a few key currencies is not and cannot be a broad program of relief from foreign competition. Rather, it is a highly specific and narrow subsidy that will provide only limited help to a few producers." She asserts that the trade balance will be restored only when U.S. industries regain international competitiveness through increased productivity and greater efficiency.[10] Economist Michael Hudson has pointed out that the benefits of a cheap dollar are limited. He has maintained that "the really important variables in the comparative trade advantages of countries are their labor costs, interest rates and tax obligations." Hudson argues that as automation becomes more and more widespread, production will depend more on capital and financing and less on the cost of labor. The problem, he says, with policymakers is that they ignore these realities and choose to concentrate instead on relative currency values, which are of secondary importance—and, we would add, only a temporary, short-run solution.[11]

The crucial question now becomes: Given the seemingly inherent limitations of the declining dollar strategy (currency devaluation) of the United States and the other G-7 countries, is there a workable strategy for the coordination of exchange rates among the G-7 countries that would resolve the problem of trade imbalance?

Exchange Rate Coordination

The one significant result of the Tokyo Summit of 1986 was a tacit agreement among the G-7 countries to construct an indicator system to help guide the international coordination of macroeconomic policies. This agreement was informal and voluntary, but it was a step toward a mechanism to set target zones for exchange rates. Although a follow-up meeting in Paris (the Louvre Accord) in February 1987 called for the further development of and a commitment to such an indicator system, it became readily apparent that a more formal mechanism was needed by which to establish agreed-upon parameters (target zones) between which exchange rates could fluctuate.

Since the Plaza Agreement in 1985, the G-7 nations have engaged in a form of international exchange rate coordination that has been largely based upon interventionist actions on the part of central banks rather than on a systematic assessment of domestic macroeconomic policy coordination. For the United States, international monetary policy has essentially involved direct intervention in exchange markets by the Federal Reserve and the manipulation of interest rates to control the decline of the U.S. dollar.

Thus, the dollar debate has been reduced to a discussion of how low the dollar should be allowed to fall, how fast, and how far. But at the same time the dollar has been held hostage by the trade deficit and the budget deficit. The lesson is that it is vital to understand that any reconstruction of the international monetary system will of necessity require a formal method and system for setting and maintaining stability in foreign exchange markets. This means going beyond discretionary interventionism and monetary policy. This policy, for example, forced foreign central banks to buy $115 billion (net) U.S. dollars between November 1986 and November 1987. These were, in essence, unwanted dollars that represented loans to the U.S. Treasury to finance the U.S. deficit. This, as Paul Farba, a columnist for *Le Monde,* has argued, is a hidden danger of such currency cooperation because it indirectly fuels U.S. consumers' purchasing power to buy imports and does not contribute to a systematic or structural solution to the continued instability of exchange rates.[12]

As part of a newly conceived international monetary system, it will be necessary to go beyond informal indicators and loose policy coordination. Several such systems have been proposed.

Proposals for Exchange Rate Coordination

Ronald I. McKinnon, an economist from Stanford University, has proposed versions of a basic model for currency cooperation. He argues that a trade deficit is not a monetary phenomenon; instead, it indicates that an economy is saving too little or investing too much. In the case of the United States, he (as have many others) identifies the problem as being too large a federal deficit.

For McKinnon the central question is one of being able to establish exchange rates without having to drive the dollar up and down with monetary policy. Therefore he proposes that the Western World adopt a system of purchasing power parity (PPP) as a theoretical guide for central banks and financial markets. Such a benchmark would allow for the calculation of nominal exchange rates that would align national price levels of internationally tradable goods as measured by producer price indexes. These exchange rates—within narrow bands—would serve as the official exchange rate target range for governments.

Under such a scheme, international trade and mutual monetary adjustment would ensure convergence to the same rate of commodity price inflation. Eventually, McKinnon argues, tradable goods' prices would then be aligned, and relative growth in national money claims would reflect differentials in productivity growth.

How would such a system be coordinated? McKinnon suggests that the country with a weak currency would slow its domestic money growth, if necessary raising short-term interest rates relative to those abroad, while monetary policy in the strong currency market became more expansionary. Thus, the aggregate money stock remains unchanged. Although the mechanics of such a system are more complicated than spelled out here, it is clear that such a system could be operationalized without great difficulty if a general agreement could be reached.[13]

Similar proposals, developed by John Williamson, an economist with the Institute for International Economics, calls for the establishment of international macroeconomic policy coordination in a manner that transcends anything the G-7 countries have done to date. The primary goal of such coordination is to maintain as high a level of economic growth as possible while avoiding excessive inflation and disruptive destabilizing financial disequilibrium—especially excessive trade and budget deficits. The Williamson proposal calls for the determination of target zones for exchange rates for each of the major G-7 countries. Such target zones would be mutually consistent with the internal domestic policies of each country. The basic policy objectives of increasing growth, lowering inflation, increasing employment, and balancing payments would of necessity have to reflect normal timing lags.

In order to implement such a program, it would be necessary to set targets for exchange rates and the rate of growth of nominal domestic demand. The exchange rate, the central determinant of the division of demand between domestic and foreign sources and of supply between domestic and foreign markets, is, Williamson argues, the central determinant of the current account. Thus, to have a target for the current account means having a target for the exchange rate. Such a target must also focus on the real effective exchange rate because it is this rate that is most relevant to competitiveness and the balance of payments. According to Williamson, such a target would be the fundamental equilibrium exchange rate (FEER), defined as the rate "which is expected to generate a current account surplus or deficit equal to the underlying capital flow over the cycle."[14]

To operationalize such a scheme, it is necessary to convert a target for the real exchange rate into one for the inflation-adjusted exchange rate. Following this, the need for intervention is eliminated, and monetary policy can adequately adjust misalignment if the exchange rate moves out of the agreed-upon zone by a margin of 10 percent. For the purposes of making policy, this would require managing interest rates and overall fiscal policy in each country to achieve the targets for a set of growth rates of nominal domestic demand and (mutually consistent) real effective exchange rates. In order to accomplish these objectives, Williamson proposes that all participants would have to agree to modify their monetary and fiscal policies according to the following principles:

1. The average level of world (real) short-term interest rates should be revised up (down) if aggregate growth of nominal income is threatening to exceed (fall short of) the sum of the target growth of nominal demand for the participating countries.
2. Differences in short-term interest rates among countries should be revised when necessary to supplement intervention in the exchange markets to prevent the deviation of currencies from their target ranges.
3. National fiscal policies should be revised with a view to achieving national target rates of growth of domestic demand.

The proponents of such an approach to the coordination of exchange rates have utilized simulations of such policies for the G-7 countries to demonstrate that if such an indicator system had been adopted between 1980 and 1987, the instability experienced would have been essentially eliminated.

It is important to note that all efforts designed to expand and operationalize mechanisms for exchange rate coordination and overall international economic cooperation assume that the participants will be willing to sacrifice some national sovereignty.

A World European Monetary System?

Experts such as France's minister of finance, Edouard Balladur, have proposed that a world version of the European Monetary System (EMS) might provide a guide to the future. Like the EMS, it would provide for automatic trigger mechanisms and appropriate sanctions. An EMS model would require a monetary reference unit determined by a weighted average of international currencies that would serve as the standard for such a new system. Under such a system, each nation would be required to adhere to margins of fluctuations set around the target rate defined for each currency. Thus, each central bank would have to be prepared to intervene in exchange markets to ensure that its currency did not exceed its limits.

The obligation to intervene to maintain the value of its currency would force each country's central bank either to spend its reserves or borrow from its trading partners when necessary. These required changes in reserves would be an indirect sanction. If it were necessary to redefine the current currency standard (parity realignment) fundamentally, this could occur only with the mutual consent of all.

The all-important difference between such a system and the old Bretton Woods arrangement is that the beleaguered U.S. dollar—now the world's key currency—would be replaced by a world currency. Thus the redefinition of the role of the U.S. dollar is one of the most important considerations related to the reconstruction of the international monetary system. Hence, it should be among the top priorities at a new Bretton Woods conference.[15]

The eventual resolution of the crisis of imbalance will require that, in addition to the basic areas of trade and exchange rates, the problem of Third World external debt must be confronted. The central challenge here is to devise an approach that offers genuine debt relief to the overindebted nations while allowing for the growth and stability of the world economy simultaneously—a tall order but not impossible.

Third World Debt Relief

By 1987 the external liabilities of developing countries had reached over $1 trillion. By the early 1980s the problem (especially for the major debtors) had become a debt-service burden that resulted in the net transfer of capital from the debtor countries to the creditor countries. This reverse capital flow has made it virtually impossible for nations to find the resources necessary to promote balanced domestic economic growth. The need to service debt has forced the debtor nations into transforming their economies into open-export-oriented economies with increased emphasis on market solutions for their economic problems. This adjustment and restructuring, which seems necessary because of current arrangements, has not been without serious consequences. Third World standards of living have steadily declined even though, on the surface, balance of trade conditions appear to have improved.

While the Reagan administration's commitment to the Baker plan (the banks' continuing to finance interest payments to themselves) appears to be unwaivering, many experts view it as having been unsuccessful and insufficient. Critics maintain that the Third World debt problem is one of structural overindebtedness; it is a long-run solvency problem rather than a short-run problem. Virtually all of the private commercial banks seem to agree since they have in recent years drastically reduced the level of new loans to debtor nations (table 3–1). It is also clear that they have begun to recognize that they need to prepare for the time when they will have to accept large losses because the loans will never be paid back. In anticipation, many banks have increased their loan-loss reserves, money set aside to cover potential losses on their Third World loans, to enable them to reduce their total debt exposure to levels that are more realistic in terms of potential repayment (table 3–2). Such losses will inevitably reduce bank equity and capital base. This eventually will be reflected in the bank stock prices and profits.[16]

Table 3–1
Debt Relief and New Loans, 1980–1987
(billions of U.S. dollars)

Debt Relief	January 1980–September 1987	1983	1984	1985	1986	1987 (through September)
Debt restructuring bank	321.4	43.8	87.0	22.9	72.4	84.1
Official creditors	68.4	8.9	4.1	16.4	13.6	18.8
Total	389.8	52.7	91.1	39.3	86.0	102.9
New long-term money disbursed	42.2	13.0	10.4	5.3	2.7	9.5
Concerted short-term credit facilities	36.2	29.4	34.9	32.0	31.5	31.1

Source: World Bank, *World Debt Tables,* I (Washington, D.C.: World Bank, 1988), p. 22.

Viewing the developing country debt problem as one of solvency means seriously considering ways in which it is possible to develop a solution that produces concessionary debt relief. Debt relief requires that debt-servicing requirements be significantly reduced so that debtor countries can again begin to generate a positive capital inflow from the advanced creditor nations. Such flows are vital if the debtor nations are to have any chance of developing balanced sustainable economic growth and improvements in their standards of living, which are now sliding backward.

Table 3–2
Big Lenders to Developing Countries
(billions)

	Loans to LDCs	Added to Loss Reserves	1987 Earnings (Loss)	1986 Earnings (Loss)
Citibank	$15.59	$3.0	$1.06	($1.00)
BankAmerica	10.00	1.1	(0.52)	(0.75)
Manufacturers	8.4	1.7	0.41	(1.05)
Chase	8.7	1.6	0.59	(0.85)
J.P. Morgan	6.0[a]	[b]	0.87[a]	0.92[a]
Chemical	5.9	1.1	0.40	(0.71)
Bankers Trust	4.0	0.7	0.43	(0.18)
First Chicago	2.8	0.8	0.28	(0.44)
Security Pacific	1.9	0.5	0.39	0.15
Wells Fargo	1.9	[b]	0.27	0.33[a]
First Interstate	1.6	0.75	0.34	(0.20)

Source: Morgan Guaranty & Trust Company, 1987.
[a]Estimated.
[b]Nothing added so far in 1987.

There are numerous debt-relief proposals. Most, however, involve at least one or some combination of the following five categories:

1. Canceling part of the debt or declaring a moratorium on payments for a stipulated period of time.
2. Subsidizing interest rates or reducing real interest rates.
3. Capping interest rates on variable-rate loans or issuing variable maturity loans that become operative when the interest rate exeeds some predetermined limit set in relationship to measurable indicators such as the debt service-to-export ratio.
4. Capping the percentage of export earnings to be devoted to servicing foreign debt.
5. Enabling developing nations to convert part of their short- and medium-term debts into longer-term obligations.

One of the more imaginative plans has been detailed by Morris Miller, who argues for a comprehensive debt policy that would guarantee debt relief by the rescheduling of principal payments coupled with reductions in real interest rates so that the overall debt servicing burden is significantly reduced.[17]

Miller, however, emphasizes that while significantly reducing the debt servicing burden is vital, it alone is not enough. Net capital must flow to the debtor nations as well. The unlikelihood that this will occur through an expansion of private commercial bank loans, he feels, requires that the World Bank increase the capital resources available for debtor nations and additionally liberalize the conditionality requirements of the World Bank's structural adjustment loans. Miller also wants the IMF to support debtor nation domestic economic policies that are growth oriented as opposed to austerity driven. He thus agrees with John Loxley, who has summarized how such an approach might work:

> [Such a] policy package would be tailored to the specific structural characteristics of the economy in question. It would rely more on selective policy instruments designed to influence behaviour in particular sectors or industries than on blunt instruments designed to have an economy-wide impact. It would favour gradual shifts in policy over shock treatment. It would be more sensitive to distributional implications and especially to the importance of preserving and/or extending the provision of basic needs, goods and services. Above all it would seek to establish broad political support for adjustment efforts thereby maintaining, or even strengthening, democratic institutions. Such a package would undoubtedly imply less reliance on unfettered market forces and greater use of selective direct controls (including exchange controls, import controls, some price control and a general incomes policy) than would orthodox packages. It would avoid a blanket commitment to an

outward-oriented economy. It would put national economic integration and the meeting of basic needs to the forefront of economic strategy.[18]

Loxley's alternative stabilization approach assumes that the debtor countries will undergo significant internal adjustment and economic restructuring but in a way that allows for diversity. This diversity, he argues, should reflect the unique character of each country and its situation.

Several noted proponents of debt relief proposals focus more specifically on the debt service problem and less on (somewhat unrealistic) overall comprehensive policies that involve the World Bank, the IMF, and debtor country responsibilities. For example, Stanley Fischer, an international economist, has made the case for debt relief on distributional (welfare) arguments. He proposes that the debt burden (interest and amortization) tied to commercial bank loans be reduced to 65 percent of the initial contracted value. This would result in a decline of approximately $10 billion a year in interest payments. In his proposal, commercial banks would gradually record these losses without serious financial consequences. However, he feels that such debt relief should be contingent upon each debtor country's agreeing to a comprehensive growth-oriented economic policy program approved by the IMF.[19]

A perhaps more realistic proposal by Jeffrey Sachs, another international economist, would have an international agency (the World Bank, for example) purchase commercial bank debt at the secondary market rate. The purchase, he suggests, could be made with marketable bonds issued by the agency. This would reduce the debt burden to 60 percent of the current amount. Sachs argues that banks could afford this because their losses have already been reflected in their stock market valuations and loan-loss reserves. As with the Fischer proposal, Sachs also assumes that the debtor nation would agree to pursue adjustment programs approved by the IMF and/or the World Bank.[20]

In the past few years a number of other concessionary debt relief proposals have been presented. Each of these involves the creditor commercial banks' absorbing some losses while facilitating an increase in capital flows to the debtor nations and/or increasing availability of foreign exchange. Senator Bill Bradley (D–New Jersey) has proposed a plan whereby commercial banks would forgive annually 3 percent of the interest and 3 percent of the principal for a period of three years, after which debtors would resume standard obligations on the remaining debt. His plan gives each debtor nation control over economic policy during this period. The commercial banking institutions of the creditor nations, not surprisingly, have refused to consider such a proposal. It is also unclear whether the U.S. Congress could constitutionally legislate such a program, and it is almost certain that the banks would not voluntarily participate. In addition, it has been estimated by William R. Cline that the Bradley plan, even if it were enacted, would do very little to help debtor nations and might even be harmful in the long run. Cline's empirical research on Mexico tends to support these conclusions. Most analysts feel the Bradley plan does not go far enough to provide any long-term resolution of the problem.[21]

Others like Peter Kenen, a Princeton University economist, Senator Paul Sarbanes (D–Maryland), and Congressman John J. LaFalce (D–New York) have each proposed versions of a plan whereby some international entity would buy Third World debt from the banks at a discount. In fact, such a proposal has recently come from a member of the IMF's executive board, Arjun Sengupta. He has proposed that the IMF established an international debt facility, which would buy portions of a debtor country's debt at an agreed-upon discount. In return IMF bonds would be given to the banks. The debtor country's obligation would be to the IMF for that portion of the debt held by the IMF. In addition, the debtor nation would have to agree to an IMF-specified economic policy program for domestic adjustment and stabilization.[22]

Many such proposals involve creative but complicated technical financial mechanisms as part of the overall debt relief strategy. Two of the more recent such mechanisms have been the debt-equity swap and the zero coupon bond option.

Debt-Equity Swap. In 1986 the volume of the trading of commercial bank foreign debt on secondary markets was about $7 billion—less than 1 percent of total developing countries' external debt. This relatively new practice has been met with some enthusiasm because of its potential toward contributing to a long-run solution to the debt problem. New interpretations of U.S. accounting and banking regulations during 1987 have contributed to this development. For example, a bank taking a loss on a sale or swap of a loan to a developing country would not be required to reduce the book value of other outstanding loans to that country, provided the bank considers the remaining loans collectible. Before 1987 that was not possible.

Many debtors whose liabilities are being traded at a discount have utilized the existence of the discount market to encourage a larger flow of private investment. The popular term for the conversion of discounted debt into local currency assets is *debt-equity swap*. In essence, a foreign investor wishing to buy assets in a debtor country can, through a debt-equity swap, obtain local currency at a discount. The foreign investor in effect obtains a rebate on the purchase of the currency equivalent to the discount on the loan less the transactions costs of the swap itself.

Chile has been one of the more aggressive users of debt-equity schemes.

Chile has a well-developed legal framework for the conversion of external debt into domestic assets. There is a similar procedure for the conversion of debt using foreign currency holdings by domestic investors.

[Figure 3–3] explains the detailed steps involved in the debt conversion. Although they seem complicated, the central steps are conceptually simple.

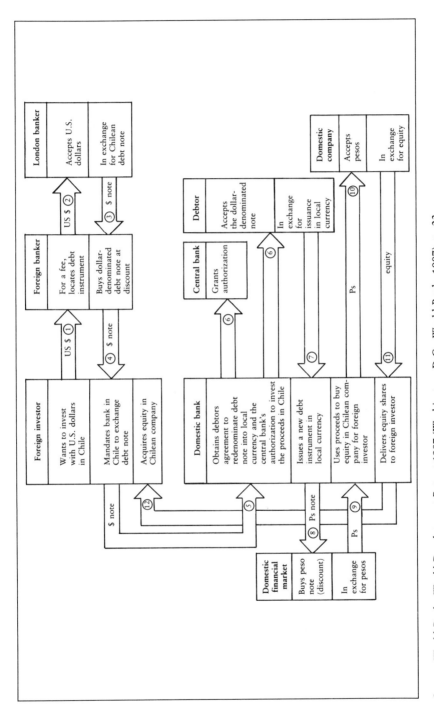

Source: World Bank, *World Development Report 1987* (Washington, D.C.: World Bank, 1987), p. 23.

Figure 3–3. Chile's Debt-Equity Swap

Debt-equity swaps are open only to nonresidents who intend to invest in fixed assets (equity) in Chile. The first step is to locate and buy at the going discount a Chilean debt instrument denominated in foreign currency. Next, with the intermediation of a Chilean bank, the foreign investor must obtain the consent of the local debtor to exchange the original debt instrument for one denominated in local currency and the permission of the central bank to withdraw the debt. Finally, the foreign investor can sell the new debt instrument in the local financial market and acquire the fixed assets or equity with the cash proceeds of the sale.

The main difference between the debt-equity swap and the straight debt conversion is that the debt conversion is available to resident or nonresident investors with foreign currency holdings abroad. Also, once the conversion has taken place, the investor faces no restriction on the use of the local currency proceeds.

The debt conversion scheme allows the debtor country first to reduce the stock or the rate of growth of external debt. Second, it is a means to attract flight capital as well as foreign direct investment. Third, debt-equity swaps imply a switch from the outflow of interest and principal on debt obligations to the deferred and less certain outflows associated with private direct investment.

For the commercial banks the swaps provide an exit instrument or a means to adjust the risk composition of their portfolio. For banks that wish to continue to be active internationally, losses on the outstanding portfolio can be realized at a time and on a scale of the bank's own choosing and by utilizing a market mechanism.

The emergence of an active market in debt instruments of developing countries offers opportunities to both debtors and lenders. There are, however, obstacles to its development. Debtor countries must ensure that transactions take place at an undistorted exchange rate, otherwise the discounts on the debt may be outweighed by exchange rate considerations. In addition, long-term financial instruments in the domestic markets are needed to ensure that the conversion into domestic monetary assets does not increase monetary growth above established targets. The incentives for foreign investors will be nullified if the broader domestic policy environment is not conducive to inflows of foreign investment.[23]

Zero Coupon Bonds: The Mexican Experiment. Mexico's external debt has grown from less than $10 billion in 1971 to over $100 billion in 1988 (figure 3–4). Mexico's rescue from near default in 1982 and another $14 billion rescue operation in 1986 have kept international bankers and governments on the edge of their seats for many years. Mexico's debt service burden has been averaging over $10 billion a year since 1985. The Mexican economy has virtually stagnated; inflation is soaring, the standard of living is declining, and the peso has steadily depreciated in value since 1982.

In an attempt to utilize a combination of the devalued peso and the secondary discounted market value of Mexican commercial bank debt, Mexican

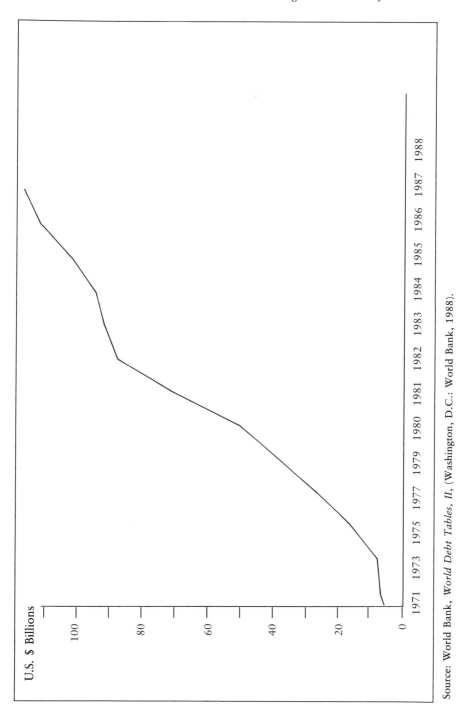

Figure 3–4. Mexico's Foreign Debt, 1970–1988

Source: World Bank, *World Debt Tables, II*, (Washington, D.C.: World Bank, 1988).

monetary authorities and J.P. Morgan and Company, in cooperation with the U.S. Treasury, devised in December 1987 a creative and unusual debt refinancing scheme. Mexico offered to swap as much as $10 billion in new bonds backed by U.S. Treasury securities for a portion of its foreign bank debt. About forty of the largest banks worldwide hold over half of Mexico's $52 billion in long-term foreign commercial bank debt. These banks were invited to bid on exchanging their Mexican loans for dollar-denominated Mexican bonds. For example, a bank may propose swapping $50 million of its Mexican debt for $25 million of the new Mexican bonds.

The principal of the bonds would be backed by zero coupon U.S. Treasury bonds, which means, in essence, that they have a U.S. government guarantee on face value and can therefore be resold in secondary markets, presumably at higher than current market rates. The U.S. zero coupon bonds themselves will be held by the Federal Reserve Bank of New York and will not be tradable. The program will cost U.S. taxpayers nothing. The cost will be absorbed by the banks, which will write off part of their Mexican loans, and to some extent by Mexico, which must pay cash ($2 billion) for the U.S. government securities that will back its bonds.

If this swap had been successful, it would have saved Mexico an estimated $18 billion in interest payments over twenty years, or about $900 million a year.[24] But this creative financial mechanism brought disappointing results. In March 1987 Mexico accepted bids amounting to $3.62 billion on foreign commercial bank debt discounted at 30 percent. Thus Mexico replaced that debt with $2.56 billion worth of twenty-year bonds. In the end, Mexico was able to reduce its debt by only $1.1 billion compared to a potential reduction of $10 billion.

The conclusion is inescapable that as long as debt relief schemes, however imaginative, are voluntary and involve banks' accepting losses, they will be generally insignificant. They will expand the growing menu of options available but will not bring about long-term concessionary debt relief. Clearly there is no shortage of ideas about how to solve the problem of developing countries' external indebtedness (see figure 3–5). The technical mechanisms and imaginative comprehensive proposals demonstrate that debt relief is possible, but until there is general agreement that the crisis must be resolved or, more likely, there is a financial crisis of major proportions, the problem will linger and continue to stifle real economic progress.

A New Bretton Woods: Conclusion

There is great need for a realignment of international priorities. To accomplish that, a new Bretton Woods conference is needed. The leaders of the world

In his statement at the 1987 Annual Meetings of the IMF and World Bank, James A. Baker III, United States Secretary of the Treasury, listed instruments suitable for inclusion in an expanded range ("menu") of financing options for commercial banks participating in rescheduling agreements. The list included the following instruments.

- *Trade and project loans,* which enable banks to channel more funds directly to the private sector. Such loans, viewed by banks as providing more easily identifiable returns, encourage imports of investment goods.

- *On-lending,* which enables banks to channel funds to specific end-users (mostly in the private sector) under their general balance of payments loan agreements with governments, thus supporting their commercial relationships.

- *New money bonds,* which are viewed by many banks as more attractive than participation in a syndicated loan as the vehicle for new money, as bonds have some characteristics of a senior claim on the issuing country.

- *Notes or bonds convertible into local equity,* which can facilitate debt-equity swaps, thus helping reduce external debt service burdens and stimulate domestic activity.

- *Exit bonds,* which are also known as "alternative participation instruments," were used for the first time in the 1987 Argentine rescheduling. . . . Exit bonds enable banks with small exposures to avoid future new money obligations by accepting negotiable low-interest bonds.

- *External debt conversions,* which are now established in many countries as a means of reducing debt and debt-servicing burdens. They permit the conversion of external claims into domestic currency denominated bonds and equity, or, in some cases, into currency itself.

- *Interest capitalization,* which reduces interest service directly. Secretary Baker indicated that mutually agreed interest capitalization may be appropriate in selected cases, particularly for small debtors.

- *Balance of payments loans,* which are the standard form for new money loans have taken hitherto. Such loans to debtor country governments will continue to be an essential component of future new money packages.

Source: World Bank, *World Debt Tables, 1988* (Washington, D.C.: World Bank, 1988).

Figure 3–5. Debt Relief Financing Options

need to come together to discuss the issues of trade, exchange rates, capital flows, and Third World debt as interrelated problems needing solutions requiring unprecedented international cooperation.

Conservative market-oriented prescriptions have not worked. Liberal structural adjustment schemes are not realistic so long as the self-interests of the banking community do not coincide with the needs of the deteriorating Third World economies and the desires of the industrialized world.

To suggest that if the leaders of the Western world come together and seriously try to resolve the problem of international imbalance seems almost unrealistic. Capitalism is, by definition, a competitive system, not a cooperative one. Beyond that the contradictions of present world economic arrangements may be too great, as Harry Magdoff and Paul Sweezy have pointed out:

> The idea that far-reaching international cooperation is feasible under these conditions is about as remote from reality as one can get. Each step in an attempt to eliminate imbalance tends to produce a new set of problems. Thus, if the U.S. were to reduce imports sufficiently to eliminate its trade deficit, the economies of countries exporting to the U.S. would suffer. This would especially hurt third-world countries who would then have even greater difficulty servicing their debts. To achieve stability in the foreign exchange markets a lid would have to be put on speculation and some means found to stabilize exchange rates. But how can stability be achieved if an exchange rate that favors one country harms another? To reap balance out of imbalance some countries would have to accept a voluntary reduction in income, leading to growth in unemployment, reduction in welfare, and a possible financial collapse. The list of contradictions could go on and on: the main point to keep in mind is that capitalism and its market system are by their very nature anarchic. To advocate eliminating anarchy—whether in domestic or international affairs—while maintaining the system serves only to foster the worst kind of illusions.[25]

4
The American Challenge:
What Can Be Done?

I n 1981 the United States emerged from the confusion and malaise of the
Carter era into a new era of optimism. The imperial presidency of Ronald
Reagan and those around him helped restore a sense of control. Reagan's
positions of dismantling the federal government, unleashing the power of
business to function in a free market setting, and reducing the tax burden on
the wealthy fit well with the age of the yuppie, the new era of greed.

To the average person looking for a panacea, Reaganomics, as it came to
be called, provided more than a glimmer of hope: it also gave new meaning
to the phrase *common sense*. Supply-side economics was supposed to relieve
the burden of taxation while simultaneously increasing federal government
revenues. The famed Laffer curve, which, legend has it, was first detailed on
a napkin in a Washington restaurant (presumably) over cocktails, purported
to prove that there is an optimum tax rate that will maximize tax revenues.
Above it taxes are a disincentive to work effort and productivity. So at any level
above the optimum, taxes should be lowered. The resulting stimulus to motiva-
tion will so energize people—since they now get to keep more of the money
they earn—that overall economic activity will boom. From that more taxes will
be collected, even at the lower rates.

This new version of "having your cake and eating it too" provided the rationale for the Reagan administration to push through tax cuts in 1981 and
again in 1986. The highest marginal tax rate was reduced from 70 percent
when Reagan took office to 33 percent by 1988. The stage was set for one
of the most important experiments in economic history.

Reaganomics meant more than just reducing taxes for the wealthy. It meant
deregulating business, cutting business taxes, reducing the rate of growth of
government spending, and "getting the government off the backs of the
American people." From this, the administration promised, the country could
expect increased productivity, more investment, more savings, lower rates of
inflation, higher real average incomes, and a growing economy.

The record, however, has been mixed. It is clear that the economy did grow,
albeit at sluggish rates, and the continuous recession-free recovery between 1983

and 1988 set new records. Therefore the proponents of supply-side economics can argue with some legitimacy that the experiment did work. However, Keynesian opponents can make a convincing argument that it was not supply-side prescriptions that were responsible for the recovery but instead the application of countercyclical Keynesian monetary and fiscal policy tools. Keynesian economics says that to stimulate the economy in a recession, the government and the monetary authorities should do some combination of increasing government spending, decreasing taxes, lowering interest rates, and increasing the money supply. In a period of inflation, when the economy is running too fast, the opposite should be done.

During the first six years of the Reagan administration, rhetoric aside, federal government spending increased from $600 billion to over $1 trillion. Interest rates were pushed down from a prime rate of 22 percent in 1981 to 9.5 percent by 1988. The money supply was increased at an annual rate of 7.8 percent, and taxes were cut drastically (table 4–1). This is the standard Keynesian prescription, and therefore, Keynesians argue, it should be no surprise that the patient recovered.

One thing is clear: the tax reduction coupled with the increase in government spending did produce historically unprecedented structural federal deficits and a national debt of $2.3 trillion, which put the U.S. economy in a precarious and fragile position, dependent on infusions of foreign savings for survival.

Table 4–1
U.S. Economic Data, 1973–1987

	Real GNP	Unemployment	Inflation[b]	Budget Deficit (billions)	Trade Balance (billions)
1973	5.2%	4.9%	8.8%	– $14.8	+ $.9
1974	– 0.5	5.6	12.2	– 4.6	– 5.5
1975	– 1.3	8.5	7.0	– 45.1	+ 8.9
1976	4.9	7.7	4.8	– 66.4	– 9.4
1977	4.7	7.0	6.8	– 44.9	– 31.1
1978	5.3	6.0	9.0	– 48.8	– 34.0
1979	2.5	5.8	13.3	– 27.6	– 27.5
1980	– 0.2	7.1	12.3	– 59.5	– 25.5
1981	1.9	7.5	10.2	– 57.9	– 27.9
1982	– 2.5	9.5	6.0	– 110.6	– 36.4
1983	3.5	9.5	3.6	– 195.4	– 67.2
1984	6.5	7.7	3.5	– 183.6	– 114.1
1985	2.3	7.1	3.6	– 212.3	– 122.0
1986	2.9	7.0	1.7	– 220.0	– 150.0
1987	2.9	6.2	3.8	– 150.0	– 160.0

Source: *Economic Report of the President* (Washington, D.C.: Government Printing Office, February 1988).

[a]Change in gross national product based on 1982 dollars.

[b]Measured by increases in the consumer price index.

It was the evolving recognition of this fact that led to the stock market crash of October 19, 1987, forcing both the government and the people of the United States to rethink the situation.

The October 1987 Crash

The crash itself, most economists now agree, was a blessing in disguise. That was less obvious at the time than it is in retrospect. The meltdown was triggered by the news that the August 1987 trade balance figures had not shown any significant improvement. Stock market analysts had long felt that the market was due for a correction, but to call what happened a technical correction was to give new meaning to the word *understatement.* The 22.6 percent market crash on "Black Monday" far overshadowed the 12.8 percent decline on October 28, 1929, that ushered in the Great Depression.

The headlines read: "TRADE DATA SET OFF MARKET PLUNGE." This was, on the surface, silly because the market had been getting bad news on the trade front for months, and the August figures actually reflected a slight improvement in the overall U.S. trade position. It was only oil imports—30 percent of U.S. imports—that were up in August. What the market reaction showed was that the underlying foundation of the overall economic situation was becoming increasingly fragile and that the market, fueled by speculative frenzy, was tremendously overexpanded.

If you are puzzled as to what a small, seemingly insignificant change in the trade data had to do with the stock market, think of it as a chain reaction that goes like this:

- The U.S. trade balance did not appear to be improving as much as most analysts thought it would. August imports exceeded exports by $15.7 billion. That was an $800 million improvement over the July figure, but forecasters had expected the deficit to fall to $14.5 billion.

- The effect was to continue the downward pressure on the foreign exchange price of the dollar.

- A weaker dollar meant U.S. investments were less attractive to foreigners because their investments here translate into fewer units of their home currency—primarily fewer Japanese yen and West German marks. Before the crash, the continuous increase of stock prices and the growth of the market had compensated for the exchange rate losses.

- A weaker dollar also means that the average price of imports rises. That helps American business to be more competitive in international markets but it also translates into domestic inflation, both directly and because U.S. businesses have more leeway to raise prices.

- This affects the stock market because investors are mostly concerned about real—inflation-adjusted—rates of return and because inflationary expectations translate into higher interest rates.

- Higher interest rates mean that bond prices fall and bond yields rise, so bonds become a relatively more attractive investment than stocks.

- Investors shift out of stocks into bonds or into cash, which means money market funds or short-term U.S. Treasury notes.

- As the market begins to slide downward, the bearish psychology feeds on itself and exacerbates the problem. Panic selling and computerized trading programs take over.

In the short run how all this affects the economy depends crucially on a number of unknowns. The one central fact to keep in mind is that except for companies trying to raise new capital, the stock market has no direct impact on how the economy operates; it is simply a place where shares of stock in existing companies are bought and sold. It is the overall level of expenditures—by consumers, by businesses, by the various governmental units, and by foreigners on U.S. exports—that determines where the economy is headed. So the real effect of the crash was to be felt indirectly, in the way it affects these variables. That leaves three key short-run questions.

One concerns the impact of the crash on businesses' capital investment plans: would it cause their expectations about the future to turn so sour that they simply stop spending? If so, the economy is headed for a recession. The second concerns the impact of the crash on consumer spending. The value of stock holdings fell by an estimated $1 trillion. Would that cause consumers to rein in their spending? If so, the economy should be headed for a recession. The third key consideration was the future direction of monetary policy. If the Fed continued down a tight money–high interest rate path, at some point further drops in the stock market seemed a certainty. So too were decreases in investment, consumer expenditures, and a recession.

By the beginning of 1988, the results were mixed. Retail sales during the Christmas season were not up but not significantly down either. In January the Conference Board's consumer confidence index was up by 7 percent. Business planned investment spending for 1988 was up by almost 8 percent, and the Federal Reserve Bank loosened the money supply and held interest rates steady. Some 50 percent of economists were predicting a recession by the end of the year.

The short-run lessons from the crash were that the stock market had been overvalued for some time, fueled by speculative frenzy. When that bubble burst, it became obvious that the market was a volatile place to invest, and many small investors pulled out. The Dow-Jones average, however, closed 3 percent higher in 1987 than it had been at the beginning of the year. Perhaps even more important was the now-universal recognition that the stock market is more closely inter-twined with the international economy that it is the domestic economy. After the crash, it became clear that what happens on the Tokyo stock exchange or in Bonn may be more important than what happens in New York.

In the longer run, the crash caused the nation, indeed the world, to move into a period of reassessment. On the practical side, the Congress and the president agreed on a deficit reduction program, which, while relatively minuscule ($32 billion), did serve to calm the financial markets and did meet the guidelines of the newly revived Gramm-Rudman deficit reduction law. Also, interestingly, the trade deficit hit a record high of $17.6 billion in November, but the market shrugged it off. To all appearances the October crash had been a correction, albeit a big one. The specter of recession remained, as did the underlying struc-tural problems, but the most important part of the crash was that it caused the country to realize that the party was over. It was, as *Business Week* put it in a cover story, time to "Wake Up, America!"[1]

One of the more significant results of the October stock market crash and its aftermath was that it spawned an unprecedented amount of literature on a topic that few had been thinking much about: where is the U.S. economy heading, and what role will it be able to play in the solution of the increas-ingly serious world economic crisis? Interestingly, a number of highly respected journalists, economists, and other commentators had been warning for some time that the day of reckoning was coming. Just before the crash, former secretary of commerce Peter G. Peterson wrote provocatively that the United States was beginning to suffer a serious hangover from its spending and bor-rowing binge—"the morning after," he called it. Also, in the summer of 1987, investment banker Felix Rohatyn warned that the Western world was "on the brink" of economic collapse; and *Wall Street Journal* economics editor Alfred Malabre penned a book detailing why the United States was living "beyond its means."[2] Before the crash, no one paid much attention to these supposed doomsday soothsayers. After it, everybody paid attention. Early in 1988 *Newsweek* summed up the national mood in a lead story: "The 80's Are Over, Greed Goes out of Style."[3]

Out of this mounting collection of literature there seemed to be an emerg-ing consensus that five major economic issues would eventually bring the U.S. economy to its knees unless some fundamental changes were made:

1. Conservatives and liberals alike agree that the United States has been spend-ing far beyond its means. If it continues to do so, the country faces a substantial externally imposed reduction in its standard of living, possibly of depression proportions.

2. The United States cannot keep borrowing from abroad to finance its lavish life-style. If it does, it will face the prospect of becoming a second-rate power.

3. Import consumption has to be reduced, and the export sector has to become more efficient. If the United States is to maintain even a semblance of world economic leadership, it has to become more competitive. Current improvements in productivity will not be enough to keep Japan, West Germany, and many others from catching up soon.

4. The Third World debt problem must be resolved. Otherwise these impoverished nations will fall into a domino-like default that will drag everyone into a quagmire.

5. The role of the U.S. dollar as the anchor currency of the international financial system has to be reevaluated. The United States cannot be the world's largest debtor and also continue acting as if it could be the lender of last resort.

The Emerging Agenda

Out of this recognition that these problems must be resolved in the long run has come a general consensus about what policies will need to be implemented.

First, spending has to be cut on most fronts or revenues must be increased. The major issue is that spending cannot realistically be cut until the built-in escalators in the programs that people have come to think they are entitled to (such as annual cost of living increases in social security and federal pensions) and exorbitant defense expenditures are revised to reflect modern realities. This is difficult and complicated and will no doubt create hardships, but so will the alternatives. In the private sector, levels of consumption have to be reduced and saving increased. If this does not happen, the falling value of the dollar will do it instead by making imports prohibitively expensive and kicking off inflation in the process. If we consume less, we will, by definition, save more. The issue here is that such measures—as attractive as they seem in a rhetorical sense—involve trade-offs and questions of equity and burden sharing. If entitlements are reduced, the poor and middle class will sacrifice the most. This is not easy to recommend, nor is it likely to be politically feasible. The obvious solution of increasing taxes does not appear politically feasible either given the antitax policies of both major political parties.

Second, to stimulate the sluggish economy and reduce the level of borrowing from other countries, real interest rates will have to be lowered even further. This is the best chance to avert a recession and at the same time reduce the incentive for foreigners to invest here. This step is risky and complicated but necessary.

Third, to improve competitiveness, the United States should keep trying to improve its industrial productivity, forget about self-defeating trade protectionist legislation, and try to engineer a gradual coordinated reduction in the value of the dollar while encouraging allies to lower their interest rates and stimulate their economies. A concerted domestic industrial policy and a coordinated international economic policy will be needed.

Fourth, the United States should prevail on the trade surplus countries, especially Japan, to become more involved in resolving the Third World debt crisis while at the same time implementing one of the several debt moratorium schemes that have been proposed. Otherwise the debtor countries, as Brazil and Peru have already done, will do it unilaterally. That would allow the developing countries to begin producing their way out of their increasingly serious predicament and, at the least, begin buying more of the U.S. exports they need. Everybody gains from this step.

Finally, the United States should take the lead in organizing an international monetary conference to begin restructuring the international monetary system along more realistic lines that reflect the fact that the United States is now the largest debtor nation and Japan the largest creditor and that the role of the U.S. dollar as the key reserve currency must be reevaluated.

There are those who will disagree with some of the specifics, but the emerging consensus is that this is the agenda for the next decade.

Possible Scenarios

The Short Run

In the short run the market crash and other factors that have been building for some time may push the U.S. economy into a recession. If that happens, all of the problems we have delineated up to this point will be more serious than they already are and, more important, the longer-run scenarios will be exacerbated to crisis proportions.

While only about half of the economists who participate in the Egbert Blue Chip Consensus Forecast thought that the market crash would bring on a recession in 1988, most do think that the U.S. economy is long overdue for a downturn and that it will probably begin in 1989. One reason is that historically big market crashes have always preceded recessions. The market has fallen by 30 percent or more eleven times since 1885, and each time a recession has followed within a year or so.

A recession in itself is not unusual. The U.S. economy has experienced nine of them since World War II and has always managed to pull out. But this time, it will be a bit more complicated because all of the current troubles of the economy will be exacerbated. The biggest problems are the federal budget deficit, the trade deficit, Third World debt, and high interest rates. In a recession scenario each would get worse:

> There is no indication that the U.S. budget deficit will be decreased significantly, even with Gramm-Rudman in place. If there is a recession, as unemployment increases, government revenues will fall, while expenditures will increase and the deficit will skyrocket.

A recession might temporarily improve the U.S. trade deficit as imports are reduced, but that would soon reverberate throughout the world economy. As other countries lose their U.S. markets, they would also have to cut back on their imports. Everybody loses.

In a U.S. recession scenario, the already fragile Third World debt situation would become much more serious. Third World countries can service their debt only by selling more to the creditor countries than they buy, which is what they have been doing. In a recession, exports and imports on both sides would have to be reduced, making it virtually impossible to service foreign debt.

Probably most important, in a recession scenario, interest rates become a crucial unknown. Normally—if that word still has any meaning—in a recession, monetary authorities push interest rates down to stimulate the economy. But in the current fragile climate, that is virtually impossible because the United States needs high real interest rates to keep foreign investors financing the huge federal deficits. In a recession, when U.S. investments begin to look less attractive, the Fed might be forced to raise interest rates above their already high levels.

A high interest rate recession would be disastrous for the U.S. economy and the world economy as well. The alternative—a low interest rate recession and a foreign investment pullout—would be even worse because it would push the dollar into a free-fall and, at the least, take the market with it. The Fed is caught in a dilemma that seems almost unsolvable. So long as the United States is dependent on foreign savings to finance its own deficits, it will not have control of its own economy, much less the world economy.

What seems to be happening is that all of the old monetary and fiscal policy prescriptions for keeping the economy out of a recession have become neutralized by the international dimensions of the U.S. economy. One way out of this dilemma would be for the major industrial powers, especially the United States, Japan, and West Germany, to agree to a coordinated gradual reduction in interest rates. That would stimulate their economies and that of the United States and reduce the worrisome trade imbalance, but since no nation wants to relinquish significant control or perceived control of its own economy, this seems an unlikely possibility in the foreseeable future.

It is much more important than ever that the U.S. economy does not slide into a recession. Even a slight downturn could snowball into a serious crisis. More attention must be paid to resolving the longer-run problems, to keep the world from continuing to teeter on the brink of depression.

The Long Run

Earlier in this chapter we sketched the five major issues the United States must face if it is to extricate itself from the present crisis: reduce spending and/or increase revenues on all fronts, reduce borrowing from abroad, become more competitive in the international markets, resolve the Third World debt problem, and reevaluate the role of the U.S. dollar as the world's key reserve currency. If these are not implemented, the longer-run scenarios for each are dismal, if not catastrophic.

Spending Reductions. Almost everyone agrees that a reduction in federal spending is needed, but no one has any idea how, given political realities, it can be done. If it is not, the United States may well be looking at federal deficits in the $300 billion range by the turn of the century, which will result in a massive transfer of wealth from the poor and middle class to the wealthy, with all the concomitant problems associated with increasing inequality of income distribution (table 4–2).

It has become fashionable in some circles to argue that the federal deficit cannot be cut significantly because the bulk of federal spending consists of built-in entitlements indexed to the inflation rate. Entitlements, such as social security, federal pensions, and many welfare programs, when added to defense spending and interest on the national debt itself, make up some 80 percent of the federal budget. All other federal spending has been cut to the bare bone, but the budget-busting Reagan administration still managed to more than double the national debt over a six-year period. In the long run, the whole question of entitlements has to be reevaluated (tables 4–3 and 4–4).

It is useful in that respect to analyze the issue of entitlements. The bulk of the federal government's income comes from individual income taxes and social security taxes and employer contributions (table 4–5). A large portion of that is transferred back to the taxpayers in the form of entitlements (tables 4–6 and 4–7). If defense spending is considered an entitlement, then entitlement spending makes up over 75 percent of the federal budget (table 4–8 and

Table 4–2
The Tax Burden: Before and After Reagan

| | As a Percentage of Family Income | | | |
| | Income Tax Alone | | Income and Social Security Taxes | |
Family Income, 1980	1980	1984	1980	1984
$10,000	3.7	5.2	9.9	12.2
$20,000	11.3	11.1	17.5	18.1
$35,000	18.9	18.4	25.0	25.4
$50,000	24.2	22.1	30.4	29.1
$100,000	35.7	30.8	38.9	35.0
$250,000	49.5	39.2	50.8	40.9

Source: Center for Popular Economics. *A Field Guide to the U.S. Economy* (Nancy Folbre, ed.), New York: Random House, 1987.

Table 4–3
U.S. Budget, 1987–1993

Category	1987 Actual	1988 Base	Projections 1989	1990	1991	1992	1993
			In Billions of Dollars				
Revenues							
Individual income	393	390	415	454	494	533	574
Corporate income	84	99	107	119	126	130	134
Social insurance	303	330	352	380	407	433	464
Other	74	78	80	83	84	86	89
Total	854	897	953	1,036	1,112	1,181	1,262
Outlays							
National defense	282	287	295	306	320	333	345
Nondefense discretionary spending	164	175	193	202	207	215	221
Entitlements and other mandatory spending	474	497	533	572	610	649	693
Net interest	139	151	166	184	196	201	206
Offsetting receipts	− 54	− 55	− 58	− 61	− 63	− 66	− 69
Total	1,005	1,005	1,129	1,203	1,269	1,332	1,393
Deficit	150	157	176	167	158	151	134
			As a Percentage of GNP				
Revenues							
Individual income	8.9	8.3	8.3	8.5	8.7	8.8	8.8
Corporate income	1.9	2.1	2.1	2.2	2.2	2.1	2.1
Social insurance	6.9	7.1	7.1	7.1	7.2	7.1	7.1
Other	1.7	1.7	1.6	1.6	1.5	1.4	1.4
Total	19.4	19.2	19.1	19.4	19.5	19.4	19.4
Outlays							
National defense	6.4	6.1	5.9	5.8	5.6	5.5	5.3
Nondefense discretionary spending	3.7	3.7	3.9	3.8	3.6	3.5	3.4
Entitlements and other mandatory spending	10.8	10.6	10.7	10.7	10.7	10.7	10.7
Net interest	3.1	3.2	3.3	3.4	3.4	3.3	3.2
Offsetting receipts	− 1.2	− 1.2	− 1.2	− 1.1	− 1.1	− 1.1	− 1.1
Total	22.8	22.5	22.7	22.6	22.3	21.9	21.5
Deficit	3.4	3.4	3.5	3.1	2.8	2.5	2.1

Source: Congressional Budget Office, *The Economic and Budget Outlook: Fiscal Years 1989–1993,* February 1988.
Note: Totals include social security revenues and outlays, which are off-budget.

Table 4–4
U.S. Budget: Revenues, Outlays, and Deficits
(billions)

Fiscal Year	Total Revenues	Total Outlays	Deficit (−) or Surplus	Debt Held by the Public
1962	99.7	106.8	−7.1	248.4
1963	106.6	111.3	−4.8	254.5
1964	112.6	118.5	−5.9	257.6
1965	116.8	118.2	−1.4	261.6
1966	130.8	134.5	−3.7	264.7
1967	148.8	157.5	−8.6	267.5
1968	153.0	178.1	−25.2	290.6
1969	186.9	183.6	3.2	279.5
1970	192.8	195.6	−2.8	284.9
1971	187.1	210.2	−23.0	304.3
1972	207.3	230.7	−23.4	323.8
1973	230.8	245.7	−14.9	343.0
1974	263.2	269.4	−6.1	346.1
1975	279.1	332.3	−53.2	396.9
1976	298.1	371.8	−73.7	480.3
1977	355.6	409.2	−53.6	551.8
1978	399.6	458.7	−59.2	610.9
1979	463.3	503.5	−40.2	644.6
1980	517.1	590.9	−73.8	715.1
1981	599.3	678.2	−78.9	794.4
1982	617.8	745.7	−127.9	929.4
1983	600.6	808.3	−207.8	1,141.8
1984	666.5	851.8	−185.3	1,312.6
1985	734.1	946.3	−212.3	1,509.9
1986	769.1	990.3	−221.2	1,745.6
1987	854.1	1,004.6	−150.4	1,896.9

Source: Congressional Budget Office, *The Economic and Budget Outlook: Fiscal Years 1989–1993*, February 1988.

figure 4–1). Add to that interest payments on the national debt, which must be paid so the government can maintain its credit rating, and virtually 90 percent of the budget is locked into nondiscretionary spending.

What is more commonly considered entitlements is the social security program, which is supposed to be self-financing in the sense that workers and employers contribute to it throughout their working lives and consequently are supposed to be entitled to retirement and other benefits in their old age. The social security program is controversial partly because something in excess of 95 percent of the working population—about 110 million people—pay taxes into the system and partly because more than 38 million people—almost 16 percent of the total population—collect benefits. The program is also controversial because so few people understand how it really works.

Table 4-5
U.S. Revenues by Major Sources, 1962–1987
(billions)

Fiscal Year	Individual Income Taxes	Corporate Income Taxes	Social Insurance Taxes and Contributions	Excise Taxes	Estate and Gift Taxes	Customs Duties	Miscellaneous Receipts	Total Revenues
1962	45.6	20.5	17.0	12.5	2.0	1.1	0.8	99.7
1963	47.6	21.6	19.8	13.2	2.2	1.2	1.0	106.6
1964	48.7	23.5	22.0	13.7	2.4	1.3	1.1	112.6
1965	48.8	25.5	22.2	14.6	2.7	1.4	1.6	116.8
1966	55.4	30.1	25.5	13.1	3.1	1.8	1.9	130.8
1967	61.5	34.0	32.6	13.7	3.0	1.9	2.1	148.8
1968	68.7	28.7	33.9	14.1	3.1	2.0	2.5	153.0
1969	87.2	36.7	39.0	15.2	3.5	2.3	2.9	186.9
1970	90.4	32.8	44.4	15.7	3.6	2.4	3.4	192.8
1971	86.2	26.8	47.3	16.6	3.7	2.6	3.9	187.1
1972	94.7	32.2	52.6	15.5	5.4	3.3	3.9	207.3
1973	103.2	36.2	63.1	16.3	4.9	3.2	3.6	230.8
1974	119.0	38.6	75.1	16.8	5.0	3.3	5.4	263.2
1975	122.4	40.6	84.5	16.6	4.6	3.7	6.7	279.1
1976	131.6	41.4	90.8	17.0	5.2	4.1	8.0	298.1
1977	157.6	54.9	106.5	17.5	7.3	5.2	6.5	355.6
1978	181.0	60.0	121.0	18.4	5.3	6.6	7.4	399.6
1979	217.8	65.7	138.9	18.7	5.4	7.4	9.3	463.3
1980	244.1	64.6	157.8	24.3	6.4	7.2	12.7	517.1
1981	285.9	61.1	182.7	40.8	6.8	8.1	13.8	599.3
1982	297.7	49.2	201.5	36.3	8.0	8.9	16.2	617.8
1983	288.9	37.0	209.0	35.3	6.1	8.7	15.6	600.6
1984	298.4	56.9	239.4	37.4	6.0	11.4	17.0	666.5
1985	334.5	61.3	265.2	36.0	6.4	12.1	18.5	734.1
1986	349.0	63.1	283.9	32.9	7.0	13.3	19.9	769.1
1987	392.6	83.9	303.3	32.5	7.5	15.0	19.3	854.1

Source: Congressional Budget Office, *The Economic and Budget Outlook: Fiscal Years 1989–1993*, February 1988.

Table 4–6

U.S. Outlays for Major Spending Categories, Fiscal Years 1962–1987
(billions)

Fiscal Year	National Defense	Entitlements and Other Mandatory Spending	Nondefense Discretionary Spending	Net Interest	Offsetting Receipts	Total Outlays
1962	52.3	30.5	24.1	6.9	−7.0	106.8
1963	53.4	33.0	25.3	7.7	−8.1	111.3
1964	54.8	34.3	29.1	8.2	−7.8	118.5
1965	50.6	34.5	32.5	8.6	−8.0	118.2
1966	58.1	37.2	38.4	9.4	−8.5	134.5
1967	71.4	45.0	41.1	10.3	−10.3	157.5
1968	81.9	52.1	43.8	11.1	−10.8	178.1
1969	82.5	58.4	41.2	12.7	−11.1	183.6
1970	81.7	66.2	45.1	14.4	−11.6	195.6
1971	78.9	80.6	50.1	14.8	−14.2	210.2
1972	79.2	94.2	56.0	15.5	−14.2	230.7
1973	76.7	110.3	59.5	17.3	−18.1	245.7
1974	79.3	124.0	65.9	21.4	−21.3	269.4
1975	86.5	155.8	83.3	23.2	−18.5	332.3
1976	89.6	182.2	93.0	26.7	−19.7	371.8
1977	97.2	197.2	106.5	29.9	−21.6	409.2
1978	104.5	217.5	124.3	35.4	−23.0	458.7
1979	116.3	235.7	134.8	42.6	−26.1	503.5
1980	134.0	278.2	156.6	52.5	−30.3	590.9
1981	157.5	321.0	170.3	68.7	−39.3	678.2
1982	185.3	357.5	155.1	85.0	−37.2	745.7
1983	209.9	399.0	157.5	89.8	−47.8	808.3
1984	227.4	394.8	165.7	111.1	−47.2	851.8
1985	252.7	437.8	175.8	129.4	−49.5	946.3
1986	273.4	455.4	174.1	136.0	−48.6	990.3
1987	282.0	474.1	163.9	138.6	−54.1	1,004.6

Source: Congressional Budget Office, The Economic and Budget Outlook: Fiscal Years 1989–1993, February 1988.

What is commonly called "social security" is four separate programs, each financed by its own trust fund. The oldest and largest, created in 1935, is the Old Age and Survivors Insurance program (OASI). The main beneficiaries of this program, financed by the OASI, are retired workers and their dependents and the survivors (spouses and children up to the age of 18) of deceased workers. It paid benefits of $183.6 billion in 1987. The second program, created in 1956, is the Disability Insurance (DI) program, which pays benefits to disabled workers and their dependents. It is the smallest program, paying $20.5 billion in benefits in 1987, and is financed by the DI trust fund. The newest programs, created in 1965, are Hospital Insurance (HI) and Supplementary Medical Insurance (SMI). The HI program pays for inpatient hospital care for retired workers aged 65 or over and for those with long-term disabilities. It paid $49.5 billion in 1987. In that same year, the SMI program paid $30.8 billion for

Table 4–7
U.S. Outlays for Entitlements, Fiscal Years 1962–1987
(billions)

Fiscal Year	Medicaid	Other Means-Tested Programs	Social Security	Medicare	Other Retirement and Disability	Unemployment Compensation	Other Non-Means-Tested Programs	Total Entitlements and Other Mandatory Spending
1962	0.1	4.2	14.1	—	2.6	3.5	5.9	30.5
1963	0.2	4.6	15.5	—	2.9	3.6	6.3	33.0
1964	0.2	4.8	16.3	—	3.3	3.4	6.3	34.3
1965	0.3	5.0	17.1	—	3.5	2.7	5.9	34.5
1966	0.8	5.0	20.2	0.0	4.1	2.2	4.9	37.2
1967	1.2	5.0	21.3	3.2	4.8	2.3	7.2	45.0
1968	1.8	5.7	23.0	5.1	5.7	2.2	8.7	52.1
1969	2.3	6.4	26.5	6.3	5.2	2.3	9.4	58.4
1970	2.7	7.4	29.4	6.8	6.6	3.1	10.2	66.2
1971	3.4	10.0	34.8	7.5	8.2	5.8	10.9	80.6
1972	4.6	11.7	39.0	8.4	9.5	6.7	14.3	94.2
1973	4.6	11.5	47.9	9.0	11.5	4.9	21.0	110.3
1974	5.8	13.9	54.5	10.8	13.6	5.6	19.8	124.0
1975	6.8	18.9	63.1	14.1	16.4	12.8	23.6	155.8
1976	8.6	22.2	72.2	17.0	18.6	18.6	25.1	182.2
1977	9.9	24.0	83.2	20.7	21.2	14.3	24.0	197.2
1978	10.7	25.3	91.8	25.0	23.2	10.8	30.7	217.5
1979	12.4	27.1	101.9	28.9	27.3	9.8	28.4	235.8
1980	14.0	32.6	117.1	33.9	31.5	16.9	32.2	278.2
1981	16.8	37.8	138.0	41.3	36.6	18.3	32.2	321.0
1982	17.4	38.1	154.1	49.2	39.8	22.2	36.7	357.5
1983	19.0	40.6	168.6	55.5	41.9	29.7	43.6	399.0
1984	20.1	41.6	176.1	61.0	43.3	16.8	36.0	394.8
1985	22.7	43.7	186.5	69.8	44.0	15.8	55.4	437.8
1986	25.0	45.9	196.7	74.2	46.7	16.1	50.7	455.4
1987	27.4	46.5	205.2	79.9	49.2	17.1	48.9	474.1

Source: Congressional Budget Office, *The Economic and Budget Outlook: Fiscal Years 1989–1993*, February 1988.

Table 4–8
Reagan Spending Priorities

	1980	1987
Military national defense (veterans' benefits)	26%	30%
Social programs	35	28
Social Security and Medicare	26	28
Net interest	9	14
Other	5	1

Source: Center for Popular Economics, *A Field Guide to the U.S. Economy, 1987* (Nancy Folbre, ed.), New York: Random House, 1987.

physicians' services, outpatient hospital services, and related medical expenses for those over 65 and the long-term disabled. Together these last two programs are known as Medicare.

The OASI, DI, and HI trust funds are fed by a payroll tax of 7.51 percent, currently paid on earnings up to $45,000. The maximum amount an employee can pay is $3,375, and that is matched by an additional contribution of $3,375 made by employers. The SMI program is financed by voluntary contributions made by the insured that are supposed to be sufficient to cover the program's expenses.

Each year the board of trustees of the OASI and DI trust funds and of the Medicare trust funds issue reports on the financial status of the funds and on projections of revenues and expenditures for the next seventy-five years. Projections made in the early 1980s showed that the program would go broke soon if something did not change. These projections prompted President Reagan to appoint a commission (the Greenspan commission) to study ways to improve the program's financial future. Out of that came a series of changes that boosted income and trimmed some benefits, all aimed at getting the program ready to accommodate the onslaught of baby-boomer retirees coming along in about thirty years.

The social security program should be in solid shape well into the next century. After that, the population trends seem to indicate, as more people retire earlier and live longer, it will again be in a crisis. In 1960 there were 5.1 people working and paying taxes for each beneficiary. By 1986 that number had dropped to 3.4, and it is estimated to fall to only 2 workers supporting each beneficiary by 2030. Clearly the programs would not be sustainable at that level. Some changes will have to be made. This long-run trend, as opposed to the short-run surpluses, concerns many economists. Former commerce secretary Peter Peterson has summed up the situation eloquently:

> Over the longer term . . . entitlement benefits dominate the picture. Since 1965 they have grown from 5.4 percent or 11.5 percent of GNP; all other spending excluding interest . . . has declined from 11.0 percent to 9.5 percent of GNP.

$ Billions

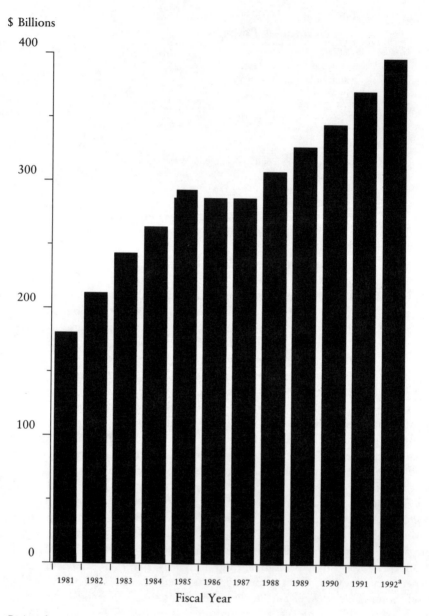

Fiscal Year

^aProjected

Source: Congressional Budget Office, *An Analysis of the President's Budgetary Proposals for Fiscal Year 1989*, March, 1988.

Figure 4–1. The Reagan Military Buildup

This growth in entitlements over the past twenty-one years is equivalent to 6.1 percent of GNP—an amount greater than the entire investment we currently make in all business plant and equipment, plus all civilian R & D, plus all public infrastructure.[4]

No one would argue that the poor and less fortunate and even the middle class should have the benefits they currently receive reduced. But that is not the issue. As Peterson makes clear:

> How much of all this spending went toward alleviating poverty? No one knows for certain, but probably no more than about 20 percent of the total, or approximately $100 billion. The rest represents income transfers from non-poor taxpayers to non-poor beneficiaries (and, increasingly, to non-poor purchasers of federal debt).
>
> This result should not be surprising, considering that of the $455 billion dispensed from the federal budget, 85 percent was not means-tested—in other words, was not targeted to people living in poverty. These non-means-tested benefits went, by and large, to those groups least likely to be poor. Far from targeting the poor, Social Security cash benefits are actually regressive, in the sense that those with the highest life-time incomes receive the highest monthly payments.[5]

This means that for the long run, the current system is unsustainable. The projections, Peterson argues, are serious:

> All told, assuming that the totality of other federal costs grows no faster than our economy, the total projected federal outlays for fiscal year 2025 will amount to about 35.4 percent of GNP. Outlays for benefits will consume 22.3 percent of GNP—a sum nearly equal to the entire federal budget today—and outlays for Social Security and Medicare alone will consume more than 31 percent of workers' taxable payroll. These incredible results are most certainly not predictions; instead they are projections of the future of our present policies. That these outcomes seem impossible is a virtual guarantee that they will be just that. What they mean is that today's policies are unsustainable.[6]

Clearly in the long run, such a configuration of federal spending cannot continue. But the political realities of the budgeting process (that those receiving entitlements also vote) are such that nothing significant is likely to happen in the foreseeable future. In the international context, the United States will have to continue to depend on foreign savings to finance its deficits, which brings us to an even more unsettling scenario.

Borrowing Reductions. The United States in 1985 became a debtor nation for the first time since 1914. By 1988 total U.S. net foreign debt had reached $425 billion and was projected to top $1 trillion by 1990. In the short run this is not a major calamity for the world's largest economy, but the longer-run implications are quite another story. As Peterson puts it:

> The incredible speed of America's transformation from creditor to debtor can hardly be exaggerated. Only six years ago, at the end of 1981, the United States had achieved its all-time apogee as a net creditor, with an official position of a positive $141 billion. Over the past six years, in other words, the United States has burned up more than $500 billion, net, by liquidating our foreign assets and by borrowing from abroad. That's an immense flow of capital, even in global terms. By 1986 our net borrowing had dwarfed the fabled bank recycling of OPEC surpluses after the oil price hike of 1973 and 1979. The sum was twice the size of all foreign interest payments by all the less-developed debtor nations, and about half the approximate dollar value of total net investment in all less-developed countries combined.[7]

There are only two ways that a nation can sustain a net debtor position over any period of time. One is to maintain a balance-of-trade surplus, thereby earning sufficient foreign exchange in its merchandise and service trade accounts to finance its deficit in the investment account. This is one way to keep the overall current account in balance, and it is what the United States did for most of the postwar period when both the trade and the investment accounts were positive. The other way is to run balance-of-trade deficits but balance them from a surplus in the investment account—in other words, let the flow of foreign investments coming into the country exceed the flow going out. Since the flows are cumulative (flows of investment become stocks of it), eventually if the inflow exceeds the outflow, the recipient country becomes a debtor nation, which is what happened in 1985 when the total value of foreign-owned assets within the United States began to exceed the value of U.S. investments abroad. Part of those assets are ownership of direct investments such as factories and real estate, and part—the vast majority—come from purchases of portfolio investments (mostly stocks and government bonds). The latter help finance the federal deficit and allow levels of consumption that would not otherwise be possible.

Put differently, one country can enjoy high levels of consumption by borrowing another's savings. This, it is important to remember, is not quite the same as borrowing in the more conventional sense of the word—directly from a bank or international agency, as the Third World debtor countries have done—but the long-run result is the same: the country has to service the debt with exports, which means a reduction in its own standard of living. This is what is happening in the underdeveloped debtor countries now as they struggle to service their foreign debts, and it is what is beginning to happen in the United States. So long as the trade surplus countries, notably Japan and West Germany, are willing to continue assuming U.S. debt obligations, the situation is sustainable. But clearly there are limits to how long this can go on, and the opportunities for a smooth readjustment of this growing imbalance are, as Peterson points out, somewhat limited:

> Our opportunity for a relatively smooth readjustment is perilously narrow. On the one hand, it seems likely that the rest of the world will grow reluctant to keep lending to the United States once our net indebtedness rises much beyond 35 percent of our GNP, or a bit more than $1 trillion at today's prices. Some experts suggest that this debt may entail net U.S. debt-service payments equivalent, as a share of exports, to those of many developing nations and about on a par with Germany's reparations burden following the First World War. The experts agree that it is quite impossible for the United States to go on indefinitely borrowing principal at or near its current rate of 3.4 percent of GNP per year. Such borrowing, combined with accumulating debt-service costs, would dictate an absurd $3 trillion in net debt by the end of the century, and foreign investors would close down the pipeline long before we got there.[8]

The scenario seems improbable, if not impossible. How would the United States go about improving its export position? One possibility would be to increase agricultural exports, traditionally a major U.S. export. But Europe, and even India and China, have become net farm product exporters. The U.S. trade surplus in agricultural products has dwindled to almost zero in recent years, while agricultural subsidies still hover around $25 billion. Another possibility would be to reduce oil imports, but after some improvement in the early 1980s, U.S. oil imports have been steadily increasing and are predicted to double or triple (to $130 billion) by 1995. That leaves services, thought by many to be the eventual savior. But, Peterson points out, the vast majority of services the United States provides the rest of the world are debt services. Services that would improve the trade balance are mostly shipping, insurance, and travel, which added up to only around $50 billion in 1986 and certainly cannot be expected to increase much beyond that in the foreseeable future. We are then left with the manufacturing export sector, which, although it has shown some improvement in recent years, would have to grow at a rate of 10 percent through the 1990s to approach any semblance of balance. That hardly seems likely even under the most optimistic projections, as Peterson points out:

> In every respect the achievement would be unprecedented: we would have not only to break our earlier record but to do it with a lower average level of domestic business investment, with a complete freeze on imports, and with steadily declining living standards.
> Any way one looks at it, the arithmetic is cruel and inescapable. It's hard to image huge growth in our manufacturing output, for instance, without a very large increase in domestic business investment. But to further increase investment at home we may have to undergo a further decline in consumption, in order to hold constant our net export improvement. And, clearly, we

are not going to see any decline in consumption in favor of saving unless there is a radical change in our public policy, especially our fiscal policy and in our politics as well.[9]

Competitiveness and Productivity. Much of the overall problem facing the United States is commonly attributed to the apparent inability of the country to compete effectively against the rapidly gaining Japanese and other now highly industrialized nations. *Competitiveness* is the new buzzword. The United States has to become more competitive, it is said, and all of its problems will go away.

In one sense when people are talking about competitiveness, they are really talking about the balance-of-trade deficit. If the country becomes more competitive, it will be able to sell more abroad, which will reverse the trade deficit. But what competitiveness really means is productivity, and around that issue is a lot of confusion that must be sorted out before the longer-run implications of declining U.S. productivity can be analyzed.

Productivity is the ratio of what goes into the process of producing something to what comes out. But *productivity* is an elusive term; there are many ways to define it. Since millions of different products and services are produced and they cannot be weighed or measured to get a total, productivity is usually measured in terms of the market value of whatever is being produced. Typically, therefore, productivity is measured in terms of the value of the output produced by a worker in an hour, or what is known as output per hour worked.

Measuring the productivity of workers involved in manufacturing is straightforward. If the average worker in the widget industry can produce ten widgets in an hour and widgets sell for $1 apiece, the value of output per hour worked in the wideget industry is $10. But measuring the productivity of workers in service industries is difficult. The first problem is determining what the worker is actually producing. What is the product of an airport security guard, a receptionist in a dentist's office, or a college professor of economics? Another problem focuses on assigning some price to what has been produced. Suppose the average airport security guard averts one highjacking a day. What is that worth?

In the U.S. economy, only about one worker in five is employed in manufacturing, mining, forestry, or agriculture where they are producing some measurable tangible product. For the other 80 percent of the labor force, productivity figures are generated by assuming that the value of what a worker produces is exactly equal to what that worker is paid. If a convenience store clerk is paid $5 per hour, his output per hour worked is—according to the way we keep productivity figures—$5, and he is considered to be only half as productive as the average worker in the widget industry.

Clearly the whole issue of competitiveness as it relates to productivity is at once overworked and not well understood. Supposedly the United States is losing the trade battle because it has become a wimpering, lazy, and inefficient bunch of slobs, unable to compete with the hard-working Japanese, Germans, Taiwanese, and others. This notion has received so much publicity in recent years that—according to a survey we conducted—87 percent of college business students believe that Japan is the most productive country in the world and that the United States runs a poor third, after West Germany. This is not true. Many studies show that in terms of output per worker, the United States is still the most productive country in the world. Among them a 1986 study by the Federal Reserve Bank of Boston shows that Japanese productivity is only 93 percent of the U.S. rate of output per hour, and West Germany's is only 90 percent. There are several reasons for the confusion over this issue.

Most important is that the relative rates of productivity growth muddy the waters. To be sure, productivity growth rates in many other countries are increasing faster than they are in the United States. If present trends continue, it is possible that Japan, for one, could overtake the United States in the near future. Over the 1981–1985 period, eleven countries achieved increases in output per worker that exceeded U.S. increases. Korea headed the list with a 6 percent growth rate, followed by Japan with 3 percent. The U.S. rate of productivity growth during the same period averaged 1 percent. But present trends are not continuing. According to the Labor Department, U.S. nonfarm productivity was increasing at an annual rate of 1.7 percent in 1986.

Byeond that, looking at overall productivity figures provides a deceptive picture of what is going on where it really counts. According to the 1986 *Economic Report of the President,* U.S. output per work-hour has grown at an average of 3.8 percent, almost 50 percent faster than the postwar average and more than twice the annual average recorded between 1973 and 1981. It is quite clear that U.S. business has gotten the message: to compete in the world markets, it has to be more flexible, more conscious of worker output, less concerned with short-run profits at the expense of longer-run investments in research and development, more consumer and service oriented, more quality conscious, and so on.

But it is important to remember that in the process of making manufacturing more competitive, much of U.S. employment has shifted out of manufacturing into the less productive and therefore lower-paying service sector. That is the primary reason for the increase in manufacturing productivity. More output is being produced with fewer workers, which is what productivity is: output per hour worked.

Complicating the issue is that productivity in the service sector—which accounts for around 50 percent of U.S. personal consumption expenditures—is almost impossible to measure. And, in any case, in the contest of world competitiveness, it is the manufacturing sector that counts, not services. Services account for only a small part of U.S. exports—around $50 billion in 1986 out of $217.3 billion total exports. So the key point here is that U.S. manufacturing is not fading away as many would have us believe. Indeed the share of GNP accounted for by manufacturing has remained almost constant over the postwar period. What does count is that it is the people who are—or were—employed by it who are fading away into lower-paying jobs in the less productive and therefore lower-paying service sector. As a result, average incomes in the United States are falling at the same time average productivity is rising. In the longer run, that is the problem of competitiveness and productivity.

While much is made of the fact that total employment has increased during the 1980s as unemployment has decreased, the data, although factually correct, are illusory. Manufacturing jobs have declined during the period, while some 44 percent of the new jobs created in the service sector between 1979 and 1985 paid poverty-level wages. This, according to a study by Professor Barry Bluestone and Bennett Harrison for the Joint Economic Committee, was "more than twice the rate of low-wage job creation that prevailed during the 1960s and 1970s." Most of the reasons for this disturbing turn of events, the authors argue, are either directly or indirectly related to international factors.

> We think these developments are explained—at least in part—by plant shutdowns, foreign imports (including imports from the offshore plants or partners of American companies), subcontracting of production to lower-paying suppliers, employer mandated wage freezes and takeaways, the proliferation of involuntary part-time work schedules and personnel cutbacks associated with corporate restructuring plans. Since none of these developments is likely to change in the near future, we should probably expect the disturbing trend toward low wages to continue.[10]

Third World Debt. The other issue that will continue to haunt the United States until it is resolved is the staggering question of the $1 trillion accumulated Third World debt. There are many possible solutions, but with the exception of the Mexican zero coupon bond scheme, which has met with only limited success, there has been little progress. If anything, the problem has worsened since it first captured world attention when Mexico nearly defaulted in the fall of 1982. The key factor is that the Third World debt crisis is part of a much larger international problem of imbalance flows of trade and capital. Until those are addressed, the Third World debt issue will continue to fester.[11]

The Trade Gap and the Role of the Dollar. The devaluation of the dollar over 1985–1986 should have, according to economic theory, caused the U.S. trade deficit to turn around dramatically. It seems logical that a 50 percent reduction in the price of the dollar should translate into a 50 percent increase in the price of imports and a corresponding decrease in export prices, solving the trade imbalance problem. But in the modern world, other things are seldom equal. By 1987 the U.S. trade deficit had hit a new record high: $171 billion. This suggests that the trade imbalance problem and the concomitant dollar problem are structural in nature. It seems highly unlikely that even a further drastic reduction in the value of the dollar, which may in any case be beyond the power of the monetary authorities to implement, would resolve the problem. Given that, all of the structural changes that would be required add up to a reduction in the U.S. standard of living, at least in the short run.

At the bottom line it is becoming clear that the days of U.S. hegemony are over, and that brings into question the role of the dollar as the world's key reserve currency. At issue is the now incompatible interrelationship between domestic macroeconomic policy and international economic policy.

It is often suggested that the United States must maintain a rapid rate of economic growth and at all costs avoid a recession. But with a recession long overdue, the trade-offs to avoid one are untenable under the current unbalanced trade and investment climate. To keep the U.S. economy growing, interest rates would have to be lowered and other monetary and fiscal stimuli applied. Lower interest rates mean a reduction in flows of foreign investment that now finance the U.S. federal and other deficits. The United States is faced with a balancing act that cannot be sustained over the long run. As Michael Moffitt has pointed out:

> The United States—in part because of the policies of the Reagan administration—has considerably less leverage than it once did to apply unilateral solutions to international economic disequilibrium. The decline of U.S. power, which began in the late 1960s, has been accelerated by the twin deficits, the resulting growth of U.S. foreign debt, and, in turn, the increasing vulnerability of our financial markets. It is no wonder that the leading lights of business and politics are bemoaning the fact that the United States is now a debtor nation. Debt and hegemony do not mix—at least not for very long.
>
> With both its monetary and fiscal policy constrained by current imbalances, the United States is now dependent on the expansion of other countries' economies to keep the current recovery going. For without greater world growth, the United States will not be able to reduce its trade deficit and its accumulation of foreign obligations—indeed, they will only grow larger. Yet the United States finds it no longer has the ability to impose its will on the rest of the world and, even if it did, it is not clear that countries like West Germany and Japan could (or would) quickly take up the role of economic locomotive.[12]

Any solution must take into account and involve the interests of Japan, Western Europe, and the increasingly important NICs on the Pacific rim. Their interests are intertwined with U.S. interests in a way that is certain to change the character and structure of international economic relations.

5
The Crucial Role of Japan, Western Europe, and the Newly Industrialized Countries

W hile it is easy to argue that the decline of U.S. dominance of the world economy is a result of nearly stagnant productivity growth rates, low savings and investment rates, addiction to imports, and the resultant debt buildup, it is important to remember that the balance of world economic power would not have shifted so dramatically in recent years if it were not for the emergence of new economic power blocs that now seem certain to assume world economic leadership early in the next century. Of these, Japan provides the most dramatic example, followed closely by the European Economic Community (EEC) (table 5–1).

The Japanese Miracle

Japan, with only half the population of the United States and a total land area roughly the size of California, is challenging the United States on all fronts. The Japanese economy is the second largest in the world, and Japanese investments abroad are almost equal to total U.S. foreign investments (figure 5–1), while the U.S. economy is still three times larger than Japan's.

There are a number of theories about the causes of this economic miracle, and the literature on the topic is voluminous. Some argue that the Japanese are harder workers; others say their success comes from innvoative management techniques like the widely copied quality circles and other methods of worker involvement in the production process. Others' explanations are that they have fewer layers of management and less administrative overhead. The most common explanation, however, is that Japan (and Western Europe) got a new start after World War II when they rebuilt their industrial plant with U.S. financial aid and at the same time adopted the latest U.S. technology. Obviously there is some truth to all the explanations. But the one overriding factor is that Japanese cultural traditions are different from those in the West and highly amenable to rapid capitalist industrial development. As compared to

Table 5-1

Comparative GNPs and GNP Per Capita, 1985

	GNP 1985 ($'s)	GNP Per Capita 1985
United States	3,946,600	16,690
Japan	1,327,900	11,300
Germany	624,970	10,940
United Kingdom	454,300	8,460
Singapore	17,470	7,420
Hong Kong	30,730	6,230
Mexico	177,360	2,080
Brazil	188,250	1,640

Source: World Bank, *World Development Report*, (Washington, D.C.: World Bank, 1987).

the stereotype, Japanese culture is flexible and open to change rather than being bound by long-standing traditions that tend to stifle change and inhibit growth. More important, Japanese culture places a high value on saving and investment. Since 1960 total (public and private) net new investment in Japan has averaged around 15 percent of its GNP, compared to just over 5 percent for the United States. In 1986 net Japanese investment exceeded $300 billion annually, compared to $270 billion in the United States. Put differently, that means that in absolute terms, total Japanese investment exceeded total U.S. investment, though their economy is only one-third as large. More important, Japanese investment is financed by internal savings. The Japanese save around 17 percent of their disposable income, compared to only 4 percent in the United States. With those savings, they are adding more to their capital stock than the United States is, and they still have enough left over (about $80 billion) to finance one-third of the U.S. federal deficit.

When put in the context of longer-run trends, the future scenarios are startling. The United States and Japan maintained rough equality in current account balance from around 1975 until 1981, but from there on the trend lines diverge dramatically (figure 5-2). By 1987 Japan had a current account surplus with the United States of almost $100 billion, while the United States was running a deficit of nearly $200 billion in trade and financial transactions with Japan. Moreover, and more important in the long run, was the fact that in 1975 U.S. foreign investment far exceeded Japanese investments abroad—roughly $300 billion compared to $20 billion—but by 1987 Japanese assets held abroad had reached nearly $1 trillion compared to $1.2 trillion for the United States. At that rate Japan will be the world's largest foreign investor by 1990 or sooner.

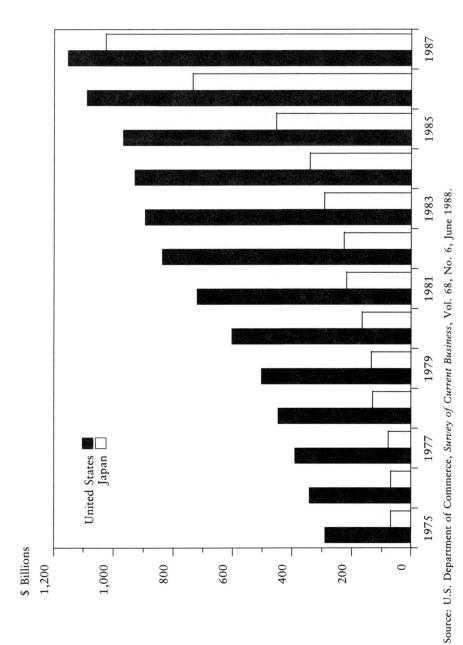

$ Billions

United States ■
Japan □

Source: U.S. Department of Commerce, *Survey of Current Business*, Vol. 68, No. 6, June 1988.

Figure 5–1. Year-End Value of All Foreign Assets Held by U.S. and Japanese Residents, 1975–1987

$ Billions

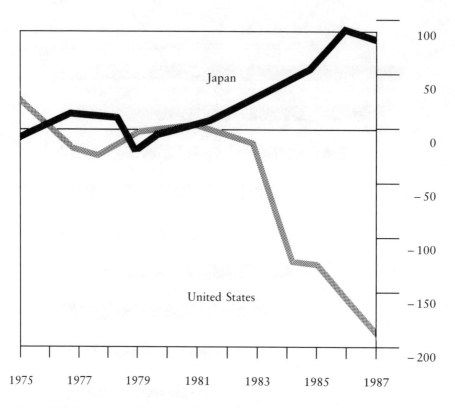

Source: U.S. Department of Commerce, *Survey of Current Business* Vol. 68, No. 6, June 1988.

Figure 5–2. U.S. and Japanese Current Account, 1975–1987

If present trends continue, Japan will become the dominant world economic power early in the next century. It is already by a large margin the world's largest creditor nation, with the power to throw the U.S. economy into turmoil at will (figure 5–3). A sudden withdrawal of Japanese investment would send U.S. interest rates through the roof and push the Western world into a disastrous recession, or worse.

Interestingly, such a scenario is unlikely because Japan has a huge stake in the U.S. economy. Some 40 percent of Japanese exports (almost $50 billion annually) are sold to the United States. Beyond that, their direct investments in U.S. companies and real estate exceed $25 billion. A U.S. recession would

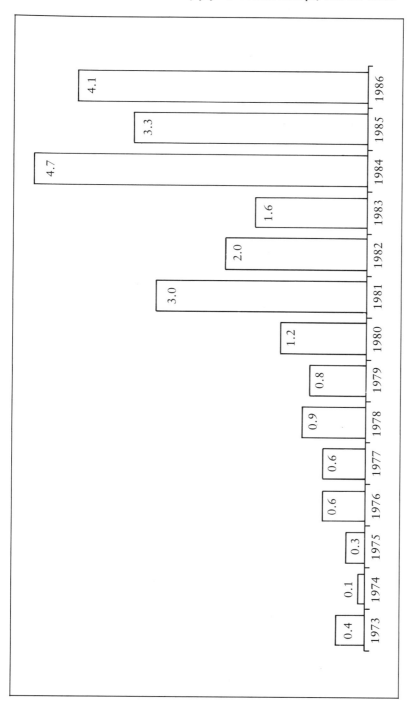

Source: U.S. Department of Commerce, *Survey of Current Business*, Vol. 68, No. 6, June 1988.
Note: Equity in and net outstanding loans to U.S. affiliates.

Figure 5–3. Japanese Direct Investments in the United States, 1973–1986 ($ billions)

send their economy into a tailspin too. In fact, trying to keep the United States out of a recession is one of Japan's biggest problems. At first glance it seemed curious that Japan would cooperate in letting the value of the dollar fall as it has since the Plaza Agreement in 1985, because a cheaper dollar means a more expensive yen, which should have made Japanese exports more expensive and turned the trade deficit around. But, for reasons we have explored, that did not happen. What did happen was that direct investments in the United States, given a dollar now depreciated by almost 50 percent against the yen, have become a bargain for the Japanese while, at the same time, adjusted for the fall in the dollar, average American wage rates became lower than Japanese wages.

This was most dramatically illustrated by the 1987 announcement that the Japanese automaker Honda was going to begin exporting cars made at its Marysville, Ohio, plant to Japan. That marked a turning point in economic history. The explanation is that Honda is able to produce the cars—which will presumably bear the label "Made in the U.S.A."—more cheaply in the United States than it can in Japan, even counting the considerable transportation costs. Part of the cost advantage can be explained in terms of the fall in the value of the dollar, since it now takes fewer yen to buy the dollars needed to buy cars produced in the United States. An equally important factor is that since 1970, manufacturing sector real wages in Japan have increased by 115 percent, while in the United States they have increased by only 17 percent. Adjusted for the fall in the value of the dollar, the average worker in Japan earned $18,000 in 1987 compared to $16,000 in the United States. It is not surprising that the Japanese are increasingly moving their production operations to the United States to exploit the relatively cheap labor.

The New Mercantilism

The Japanese economic strategy is based on two interrelated long-run policies: a return to the mercantilistic policies of Europe in the seventeenth and eighteenth centuries and a concerted effort to tie its fortunes to the United States without assuming a hegemonic leadership role.

Mercantilists believed that a nation's future hinged on its ability to produce as much for export as possible while importing as little as possible in order to build monetary surpluses (which in those days meant gold). Put differently, the goal was to export production rather than consume it. Such policies have long been discredited as, at best, a curious way to construe a nation's economic welfare, but this has been the cornerstone of Japanese international economic policy for some time.

The United States has, unintentionally, pursued the opposite policy over the past decade or so. Exports have been declining while domestic consumption, fueled mostly by imports, has been increasing. This means that Japan is rapidly becoming the world's dominant economic power, but at the same time it is becoming increasingly dependent on the United States for markets and outlets for its rapidly accumulating investment funds.

The Newly Industrialized Countries

A related and, in the longer run perhaps equally important, development is the emergence of the NICs of the Pacific rim: China, Hong Kong, Singapore, South Korea, and Taiwan. By the year 2000 it is estimated that the GNP of Japan and the NICs combined will exceed that of the United States. Already the rate of increase in exports dwarfs that of the United States, and per capita incomes are rapidly gaining (figures 5–4 and 5–5).

There are two significant issues here. One is that much of the economic growth in the Pacific rim has been dependent on increasing rates of exports to the United States. So long as this continues, an interdependent relationship

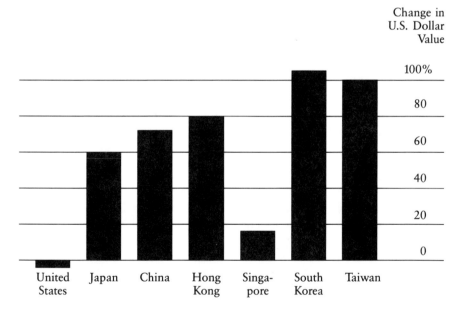

Source: International Monetary Fund, *World Economic Outlook* (Washington, D.C.: IMF, April 1988.)

Figure 5–4. Increase in Exports, 1980–1986

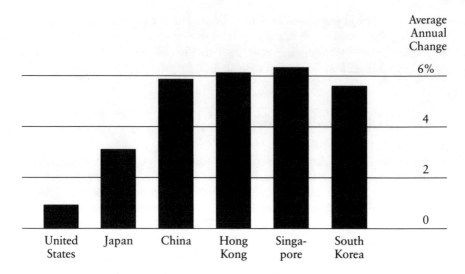

Source: International Monetary Fund, *World Economic Outlook* (Washington, D.C.: IMF, April 1988).

Figure 5–5. Increase in Per Capita GNP, 1973–1986

similar to the Japanese-U.S. symbiotic interdependence will benefit both sides. But there is an increasing trend of economic activity between Japan and the NICs that could eventually develop into a Pacific rim common market that could emerge as the dominant world economic power bloc early in the next century. When that happens, the rules of the game will have to be rewritten—again.

The Role of Hegemony

There has been no time in modern history when the international economy was not dominated and fueled by a hegemonic power. Great Britain played that role during the nineteenth century until it began to lose power after World War I. The United States played the role from the end of World War II until the end of the 1970s when it began to lose the battle of competitiveness and wallow in a quagmire of debt.

Barring an alternative system of international policy coordination, a hegemonic power can take up the slack in the world economy by providing markets for less powerful economies and by allowing, indeed encouraging, its currency to be used as a standard of value for other countries' reserves and as a medium of exchange for international transactions. It thus provides the engine of growth for the rest of the world, and, if need be, it can be the lender of last resort—the one country with the power to bail out any others that have become overextended in the international arena. The United States, to some extent, still plays that role, but it is becoming clear that the days of its hegemony are dwindling, which brings us full circle back to Japan and its interdependent relationship with the United States. Japan is not yet strong enough economically to take over the role of world economic leadership, but at current rates, it is just a question of time until it will have little choice but to assume more responsibility for keeping the world economy in balance.

Hegemony requires more than economic power, however; it also requires military power and political clout. Japan has neither, and, moreover, it shows little sign of developing, or wanting to develop, its power in either of these areas. The Japanese, partly because of limitations placed on them after World War II, spend only 1 percent of their GNP on defense, while the United States spends 6 percent. In absolute terms, the United States spends eighteen times more on defense than Japan does, leaving the burden of "keeping the world safe for democracy" primarily on the United States and, to a lesser extent, Western Europe. Japan has shown little interest, for example, in participating in U.N. peacekeeping operations or even in maintaining the free flow of oil in the Persian Gulf, though it has vital interests at stake. There is little evidence that Japan has the sense of empire required of a hegemonic power. This leaves the noncommunist world with its former hegemonic leader, the United States, with the military power but not the economic power to sustain it, and, Japan, the emerging economic power, without military power.

Divergent Scenarios

As historian Paul Kennedy has pointed out, there are two possible future scenarios.[1] One is that Japan and the United States share world leadership, with Japan providing the economic muscle and the United States providing the military power and political initiative. Under that scenario, which seems to be a primary agenda of Japanese prime minister Noboru Takeshita, Japan would increase its role in funding international organizations like the World Bank and the IMF, increase its rate of lending to the debt-ridden underdeveloped countries, open up its economy to U.S. exports, and, most important, take measures to stimulate its economy, especially domestic consumption. At the same time, the United States would continue to bear the burden of perceived mutual defense needs.

By 1988 there were signs that all this was beginning to evolve, albeit slowly. The Japanese trade surplus with the United States was beginning to narrow, Japanese domestic consumption grew by more than 10 percent over the previous year, and Japan has become a major contribution to international financial organizations. Moreover, Japan pledged some $30 billion toward resolving the Third World debt crisis. But there is little evidence that Japan wants to assume world economic leadership. Yutaka Kosai, president of the Japan Economic Research Center in Tokyo, probably expressed the Japanese feeling most aptly when he was quoted as saying: "I have mixed feelings about being a dominant economic power. . . . We hope the United States can recover and Japan will be the second fiddle. Being No. 2 is really quite pleasant."[2]

More likely, unless a new system of global economic cooperation is devised, the noncommunist world will gradually evolve into three major trading blocs, each a world within itself while trading with each other: the United States and the rest of the Western Hemisphere, Japan and the Pacific rim countries, and Europe with West Germany as its leader. This, however, is complicated by the fact that Western Europe has problems and agendas of its own that make it vulnerable to such a division.

The European Question

In many ways Western Europe provides the model for economic cooperation and policy coordination that could provide the basis for a realistically coordinated world system. The EEC, which now contains twelve nations representing 320 million people (table 5–2), has agreed to eliminate all trade barriers and trade-restrictive regulations between member countries by 1992. That will make Western Europe a coordinated economic unity almost as large as the United States and by far the world's largest consumer market. In 1987 the combined gross domestic product of the EEC was $4.2 trillion, compared to $4.5 trillion in the United States.

One of the reasons the U.S. economy is as strong as it is is the fact that the United States is the world's largest free trade zone. U.S. citizens tend to take for granted the free movement of goods, services, and people among the fifty states without any trade barriers. If you had to have a passport to travel from New York to Pennsylvania and stop for a customs check at every state border, you would have a better understanding of the European system. Each nation has its own set of regulations governing trade and, more important, its own currency, which has to be exchanged every time a border is crossed.

But this too is changing. The EEC already has adopted a coordinated exchange rate system (the European Monetary Standard), which keeps member country currencies from fluctuating excessively. And it is likely that in the 1990s, a European central bank will be established, which will operate much like the U.S. Federal Reserve System and allow for the adoption of a common currency. The Europeans have awakened to the fact that if trade barriers are removed, their economic well-being will be greatly improved and their status as a world economic power vastly strengthened. A recent study by the Organisation for

Table 5–2
Member Nations of the European Economic Community, 1987

Country	Gross Domestic Product (billions)ª	Growth Rate, 1986–1987	Population (millions)
West Germany	$1,121.2	1.50%	61.1
France	870.3	1.50	55.4
Italy	749.8	2.75	57.2
Britain	658.9	3.75	56.8
Spain	285.5	4.50	38.5
Netherlands	213.6	1.75	14.6
Belgium	139.7	1.25	9.9
Denmark	102.0	– 0.75	5.1
Greece	47.1	– 0.50	10.0
Portugal	35.4	5.00	10.2
Ireland	28.7	2.00	3.6
Luxembourg	6.2	1.75	0.4

Source: Organisation for Economic Co-operation and Development, *European Integration*, 1988.

ª1987 provisional figures.

Economic Co-operation and Development predicts that the efficiencies that will come out of the planned uniting of the European economy will increase its combined GNP by $230 trillion.

In the face of what appears to be a rapidly developing trade war, sparked by the myopic new U.S. protectionist trade legislation, the uniting of Europe stands to be one of the most significant new developments of the decade. This would be good news for the U.S. economy if a more efficient European economy was able to snap out of its current doldrums and buy more U.S. products. But it will be bad news if, as seems more likely, the EEC uses its power to erect a tariff wall that excludes the United States (and Japan) and focuses on trade among its member nations. With a home market of 320 million relatively affluent people, it can easily afford to do that.

Ironically, the 1988 trade act allows—indeed, instructs—the president's trade representative to determine what is fair trade and what is not. If a country is perceived to be practicing unfair trade policies, unilateral retaliatory measures are supposed to be put in place against the culprit nation. It is that clause in the act—the so-called Super-301 clause—that has outraged the Japanese and Europeans, who feel they are already doing everything possible to open their economies to U.S. exports.

Such a policy might make sense if the United States were still the dominant world economic power or dealing with a few small nations. But to be talking about retaliatory measures against economic powers like Japan and a united Europe is quite a different story. They can and most certainly will match

Table 5–3
Estimates of Potential Annual Economic Gains Resulting from a Europe without Internal Borders

Source of Gain	Amount (billions)	Percentage of Gross Domestic Product
Removing customs formalities	$11	0.3
Removing barriers affecting production	87	2.4
Exploiting economies of scale more fully	75	2.1
Intensifying competition by reducing business inefficiencies and monopoly profits	57	1.6
Total	230	6.4

Source: European Commission of the European Community, *European Integration,* OECD, 1988.

any retaliatory measures the United States can come up with, and the United States will not be able to respond.

The developments in Europe seem to portend the emergence of four large trading blocs that will wield tremendous economic power and make protectionist trade policies seem silly. By the end of the century, there will probably be one free trade bloc made up of Canada, the United States, and Mexico. The second bloc will contain the EEC nations of Western Europe, and the third will consist of Japan and the rapidly industrializing countries of the Pacific rim: Taiwan, Singapore, South Korea, and others. The communist bloc nations will round out the list. Each will have its own tariff walls and tremendous negotiating power. In such a scenario the idea of the United States retaliating against what is perceived to be unfair trading practices will not make any sense—just as it does not now.

The European Monetary System

One of the best currently functioning examples of how economic policy can be coordinated is the European Monetary System (EMS). Concerned about the effects of the strong dollar that had peaked during the Carter administration, European monetary authorities agreed in March 1979 to peg the value of their currencies to a common unit of account, the European Currency Unit (ECU). The ECU differs from the Bretton Woods system, which tied currencies to the value of the U.S. dollar, in the sense that it is a weighted average of all European monies; it is, in essence, a floating peg that can vary with economic conditions. If any one currency diverges in value in relation to the ECU, that country's authorities are obligated to intervene in the exchange markets to correct the imbalance and/or to make appropriate monetary and fiscal policy changes.

As a practical matter, the dominant currency in the EMS is the West German deutsche mark, which makes up over 33 percent of the weighted average. Germany's traditional aversion to inflationary policies has, consequently, been a major force in keeping European inflation rates in check.[3]

The EMS, as Michele Fratianni and others have pointed out, is, on the one hand, a system to maintain short-run exchange rate stability. In that sense, it has been rather successful. In a broader context, the EMS is perceived as a step toward economic policy coordination among the members of the EEC that would achieve parity of purchasing power for each country and provide a common standard by which their currencies could be valued against others, especially the U.S. dollar and the Japanese yen. To some extent, this has been successful, but it is not clear that it has yet stimulated trade between Common Market members or with the rest of the world.

Others, such as French finance minister Edouard Balladur, have argued that the EMS provides a model system of monetary coordination that should be adopted on the world level.[4] For a number of reasons, while such a possibility appears attractive in a utopian sense, it is probably not practical unless current trade imbalances are corrected—in which case it also would not be necessary.

One of the reasons that the EMS has been successful to a degree is that West Germany has been reluctant to fuel inflation with stimulative monetary and fiscal policy. Yet one of the major thrusts of U.S. policy prescriptions to resolve trade imbalance has been to encourage Japan and West Germany to speed up their economies in order to absorb more U.S. exports.

If Western Europe were ever to play a major role in world economic leadership, it would require the cooperation of West Germany, which has an economy roughly one-fourth the size of the U.S. economy. But only about 10 percent of German exports go to the United States, and over 40 percent go to other EEC members. To make any difference in the current world situation, Germany would have to increase its growth rates far above its 1988 level of 1.5 percent. To be sure, there is room, many analysts feel, for more German cooperation in stimulating world economic growth. German unemployment rates in 1988, for example, were running above 9 percent. But Germany has already cut taxes by $8 billion (in 1988) and another $12 billion tax cut is scheduled for 1990, and the German federal domestic deficit was $16 billion in 1988.

There is little evidence, however, that West Germany has any interest in becoming the locomotive of growth for the rest of the Western world, even if it were big enough to do so. The German population is now growing, and living standards are already among the highest in the world. And the lessons of the hyperinflation of the 1920s are firmly implanted in the German psyche. Any administration that let inflation get out of control would soon find itself out of office.

Expanding the EMS worldwide would mean that Germany would have to give up a large degree of its control over its own destiny, and that is not a likely possibility any time in a foreseeable future. That means that if Germany is not ready, the United States must take leadership in initiating a system of coordinated exchange rates. But that was tried during the Bretton Woods period and failed, and the United States has a dismal record of maintaining inflationary stability, a prerequisite for any worldwide exchange rate system. Therefore, while the EMS model has a certain theoretical attractiveness, it is not a model that could easily be expanded to the extent that it would make any significant difference in the current fragile international economic climate. So long as Japan and Western Europe are in the driver's seat, the United States will have to look for other ways out of the dilemma of its fractured hegemony.

6
Policy Challenges for the 1990s

The issues facing the global economy are becoming clearer even as politically viable policy responses become more and more nebulous. The overriding issue is that the trends in almost every sector of the U.S. and the world economy add up to an impending crisis. Even if there is gradual improvement in the U.S. trade and budget deficits, the situation is not sustainable. The primary problem is not found in the international sector, as one would expect, but in the U.S. economy. Solutions, if they are to be found anywhere, will come from initial U.S. macroeconomic policy adjustments followed by consistent and supportive policies coordinated internationally.

The Trade Imbalance

There is little reason to expect that any kind of changes in U.S. trade policy or in the policies of its trading partners would be sufficient to improve significantly—much less correct—the bleak trade picture. The U.S. auto industry had by 1988 lost 31 percent of its own market to foreign producers; 50 percent of U.S. machine tools and textiles are now imported; and the U.S. consumer electronics industry is almost totally dominated by foreign producers.

The omnibus trade bill, which after three years of negotiation and political infighting among seventeen different congressional subcommittees, became law in 1988, but there is little evidence that the myriad of so-called protectionist measures in it will do any more than placate special interest groups, further confuse the issue, and invite self-defeating retaliation. Only around 15 percent of the U.S. trade deficit can be traced to tariffs and other trade restrictions that are higher than similar U.S. restrictions against what are called "unfair trade practices" when someone else does it and "tariffs" when it is done in the United States.

Other measures to correct the trade imbalance, such as depreciating the U.S. dollar, have done little to improve the deteriorating U.S. position in the world markets. Efforts to improve U.S. productivity have been somewhat successful in the sense that exports have increased slightly but continue to be counterbalanced by the onslaught of imports. Moreover, most of the gains in productivity have come from decreases in manufacturing employment that have resulted in massive shifts into the lower-paying service sector.

The Debt Overhang

It is possible, as Wall Street economist Alan Sinai has argued, that the "twin deficits"—the federal deficit and the trade deficit—will improve slightly over the next several years, but even if they do, the specter of a growing foreign debt will continue to haunt the U.S. economy.[1] Sinai states the case bluntly:

> Though the budget and trade deficits will likely improve as a percent of GNP in coming years, the growth of government and foreign debt will continue so long as the deficits remain. Eventually, the debt and interest payments on them must be paid through less spending, more saving, and restrictions in the U.S. standard of living.
>
> The so-called "twin deficits" plus trade surpluses abroad are the fundamental problems facing U.S. financial markets and eventually the economy. The large budget and huge trade deficits that have required high interest rates to finance them now apparently require low enough stock prices as well, in order to slow the economy and release more saving.
>
> Large deficits—outlays exceeding receipts in the case of the federal budget and imports greater than exports—beget increased debt and require borrowing, for a country just as for an individual or a company. If the borrowing continues, outstanding debt keeps rising along with interest payments.
>
> The scenario by now is familiar. Huge budget and trade deficits and debt spew out a large supply of dollars relative to demand, tending to produce a lower dollar. Expected and actual inflation rise. Interest rates are pushed higher. Higher inflation hurts the dollar. The Federal Reserve is either forced to tighten monetary policy against inflation or keep interest rates high to support the dollar and to guard against inflation. If the budget and trade deficit do not improve, the process continues. Eventually, if nothing else intervenes or is done by policymakers here or abroad, interest rates must rise high enough to compensate foreign lenders for dollar and interest-rate risks and to reduce economic growth at home so that enough saving is released domestically to finance the U.S. deficits. The levels of interest rates necessary to do this are uncharted, since the circumstances of the twin deficits are without precedent in the postwar period. At some point, interest rates can reach levels that threaten business expansion in the United States and overseas, where strong currencies already may be threatening economic growth. The result then is lower stock prices in anticipation of a possible recession.[2]

Policy Proposals

There is no shortage of proposals to remedy the situation, but proposals that are both workable and politically feasible are scarce. Sinai suggests that a three-part combination of federal budget reduction and monetary policy easing both in the United States and abroad could perhaps reverse the negative trends:

> A curative approach that can cut at the heart of the problem involves: 1) a massive reduction in the budget deficits, up to $50 billion or so, with further reductions of less magnitude next year and the year after; 2) a massive offsetting monetary ease in the United States; and 3) stimulative monetary policy abroad to ease any drop in the dollar. This solution must be simultaneous—a "three-legged stool," no leg without the others.

But he admits that

> the likelihood of such a solution being undertaken must be assessed as very small, however. The odds on this grand coordination of policy, even if it is the correct policy prescription, must be regarded as very low. But, at one swipe, it would tend to relieve and probably eliminate a big chunk of the problem for the financial markets that has kept nominal and real interest rates at growth-inhibiting levels for almost all of this decade.[3]

Writing two weeks after the October 1987 stock market crash, Peter Peterson proposed that four major areas must be addressed to avoid a total U.S. economic collapse:[4]

1. Federal budget reform must be implemented through a combination of specific spending reductions and tax increases; for example, expenditures for "entitlements," especially built-in cost of living allowances in the various pension funds and increased taxes on social security benefits and other pensions, should be reduced, and a gasoline tax should be instituted.

2. More macroeconomic policy coordination will be a prerequisite for any long-term solution to be viable. The current policy of propping up the dollar by intervention in the foreign exchange markets (which amount to printing money) will lead to only more inflation and exacerbate the problem.

3. "The United States must begin to re-think how it allocates its security resources." What will be required is "a sizeable increase in the European contribution to NATO's conventional forces."

4. The time has come for a new compact with the Japanese that will involve trading security guarantees in the Pacific for a rechanneling of Japanese trade surplus earnings toward the Third World "through the [existing] multilateral economic institutions, aid untied to exports and incentives for private capital investments. Not only would this lead to greater Third World development, but it would calm fears that the debt bomb will explode."[5]

Then Peterson sums up the situation:

> At bottom, our problems are not economic. Rather, we are stymied by our lack of political consensus. We do not even agree on the nature of our economic difficulties. In Japan and West Germany, by contrast, there is widespread accord, born of national crisis, on the necessary, long-term connection between savings and investment, between investment and productivity growth, and between productivity growth and real wage increases.
>
> Historically, the American character has emphasized optimism, unfettered energy, "win-win" choices and the direct pursuit of dreams. Circumstances are now forcing us to change our behavior in a direction that has few recent precedents: toward self-denial, collective discipline, "win-lose" choices and deferred gratification. For at least a couple of decades, both in our private and public lives, we have fixed our attention on spending and consuming. Now we will have to fix it on producing and saving. Without this change, our next economic coronary could put us under for a very long time.[6]

Macroeconomic Policy

As it has become clearer that externally imposed trade measures such as protectionism and exchange rate manipulation do not and will not alter the growing imbalance of trade, it has become equally clear that the root of the problems is more a question of appropriate macroeconomic policies rather than ad hoc and ex post international economic policy responses.

If we look back at recent history, it is easy to see that the trade imbalance problem first came to public attention in the early 1980s, especially between 1981 and 1984, which was the beginning of the Reagan administration and included the 1982–1983 recession. The recession—the worst of the postwar period—was a planned part of the administration's overall economic strategy. The goal was to rein in inflation by increasing interest rates and generally tighten the money supply, while at the same time lowering taxes. This is contradictory monetary and fiscal policy, and one result was record-high unemployment rates (around 10 percent) and record-high interest rates (over 22 percent). This policy, coupled with rapid increases in debt levels, did eventually break the back of inflation, and by 1983 the U.S. economy began to recover. Since then, driven by the huge debt buildup on all fronts, the economy has grown at slow but steady rates, unemployment has fallen, and inflation has remained at relatively low levels.

During the same period, however, the trade situation worsened precipitously. The reason was partly that the Third World debt buildup effectively cut off U.S. exports to most of the lesser-developed areas and partly that the U.S. economy was growing at very high rates (7 percent), which fueled import growth without any significant increase in exports. It was this strange combination of unexpected events that caused the U.S. dollar to skyrocket in the exchange markets. Normally a U.S. trade deficit would mean a weaker dollar as dollar demand dwindled. But macroeconomic policies caused international capital flows to shift in the other direction. High interest rates in the United States, which were partly a result of the inflation reduction policies of the Fed and partly a result of the debt buildup, increased the demand for dollars, pushed the dollar up, and with it pushed the trade deficit to record levels.

There are two lessons in these unprecedented historical developments. One, as I.M. Destler has pointed out, is that

> in a world of floating exchange rates and large-scale capital flows, trade imbalances are largely immune to treatment by trade policy measures. They can be reached only by other means, mainly macroeconomic measures that influence total demand and affect the savings-investment balance within trading nations. Also, when circumstances are favorable, trade imbalances can be influenced by official intervention in foreign exchange markets.
>
> Trade measures can affect the volume of trade. They can influence the composition of that trade. But unless coupled with other measures, they will have little impact on the overall surplus or deficit run by a nation.[7]

The other lesson is that so long as the United States continues to run federal budget deficits that depend on foreign financing—that is, use foreign savings to finance domestic consumption—interest rates will of necessity remain high, the dollar will remain structurally strong, and the trade balance will continue to deteriorate. With it the international position of the United States will continue to erode. Unless something is done to reduce the federal deficit, there is little reason for optimism on any front. The net result, as the U.S. international debtor position builds, will be a gradual lowering of the U.S. standard of living as more resources are diverted abroad to service growing external debt.

Microeconomic Policy Strategies

At the microeconomic level there are numerous proposals and strategies to improve U.S. competitiveness in the international sector. Most fall under the rubric of industrial policy, which has been popularized by writers like Robert Reich and embraced in varying degrees by liberal elements of the Democratic party. There is, as Reich and others have pointed out, some confusion and misunderstanding over what industrial policy really means. In Reich's view:

> Any mention of industrial policies summons the specter of national planning, in which bureaucrats—ignorant of or indifferent to market force—shift capital from industry to industry to nurture their favorite future "winners." Our inability to distinguish between this caricature and the realities of well-designed

adjustment policies—through which government seeks to promote market forces rather than to supplant them—has confounded political dialogue.[8]

There are many ways in which business, labor, and government could cooperate to the end of revitalizing the American economy, and to some extent this is being done.[9] Even under the Reagan administration, where a strong ideological free market philosophy dominates most strategies, there has been an increasing recognition that there is a role for the government to play in improving long-run competitiveness. Indeed Reich argues the Reagan administration has in fact already implemented an industrial policy. He points out, for example:

1. In January 1987, the Administration approved a $4.4 billion plan for a superconducting supercollider: a 52-mile underground race track for sub-atomic particles. A White House official deemed the project "critical" to our future competitiveness.

2. Last July, the President announced an "11-point superconducting initiative" aimed at developing practical applications for superconducting material—special alloys that, when cooled, lose all resistance to the flow of electric current. The White House called this technology "absolutely essential to our future competitiveness." Antitrust laws will be relaxed to allow collaborative research, patent applications for superconductors will be put on a fast track, four special research centers will be established and the Freedom of Information Act will be modified to allow Government laboratories to withhold commercially valuable superconductor information.

3. In October, the Administration announced that it would fund "Sematech," a joint research venture comprising America's leading semiconductor manufacturers. "Semiconductor technology will be critical to our economic security in the years ahead," an Administration official said. "We can't afford to fall behind."

4. Last December, the White House unveiled a "high-tech" program to develop software and algorithms—all aimed at developing computers capable of performing trillions of operations per second. Warning that Japanese supercomputers were already on the market, and "with better performance than expected," the Administration proposed spending $1.7 billion over five years.

5. During the same month, the Administration awarded contracts to begin building the nation's first permanent space station. Administration officials noted that the station would be a laboratory for developing new pharmaceuticals and high-tech materials used in computers, and thus "vital to enhancing the nation's international competitiveness in the decades ahead."

And there's much, much more.[10]

Such policies are an explicit recognition that governmental policies can influence the long-run competitiveness of industry.

Labor and, to a lesser extent, business have also cooperated in the restructuring of American industry. Wage concessions by labor have permitted impressive productivity gains and held down inflation rates. Business has implemented worker training programs and instituted new, more flexible production systems modeled in large part after Japanese methods. And, more important, there is an increasing awareness that more resources have to be channeled into investments in research and development, which in recent years has been deemphasized, at the expense of short-term profits.

The key issue is that well-thought-out industrial policies are not the same as the seemingly socialistic economic planning. They encourage adjustments in all sectors toward the now commonly understood goal of and need for a revitalization of American industry if it is to survive the challenges it faces in the next decade. I.M. Destler has summed up the situation:

> We therefore need policies to speed adjustment by industry and labor, to encourage movement of resources from less productive to more productive enterprises and regions. This should be joined with efforts to increase productivity growth for the economy as a whole. There is a strong need for policies, in Charles Schultze's words, "designed to make the economy in general more flexible, more dynamic, more productive, and more capable of adjustment to technological change." Such policies need to focus on labor markets, increasing training opportunities for workers and improving market information about job openings. They can include more support of general and specialized education and encouragement of research where the benefits to society exceed those recoverable by a firm. They can include tax code changes that favor productivity-enhancing forms of investment, and that favor the domestic savings that must ultimately finance such investment. . . . The focus on our industrial productivity can be enormously constructive. It can turn American attention away from nefarious-seeming foreigners, toward self-help at home. It can focus our energies on creating an appropriate, stimulative policy environment for our productive enterprises. It can encourage a creeping recognition that many of the problems of American producers are, in important part, "made in USA."[11]

Getting Specific

How can a politically feasible industrial policy be implemented? On a practical level, it is at once complex and simple. It is simple to the extent that what has to be done is well understood; how to pay for it is quite another question. In 1986, *Business Week* outlined six areas in which change would have to be made.

First, *Business Week* financial analyst Norman Jonas suggests, the federal budget deficit must be cut so that the government stops "sopping up the bulk of private savings to finance the federal debt." This would "free capital for private investment and trim real interest rates."

Second, the tax system should be reformed in such a way that it would encourage capital investment rather than discourage it as the 1987 tax reform act did. "Congress," he proposes, "should eliminate the corporate tax entirely. This would end the double taxation of dividends and cancel the advantage of debt over equity investments. It would allow investment decisions to be made on the basis of business rather than tax considerations."

Third, Jonas says, "It's also time to repeal or at least re-write the Glass-Steagall Act to permit merchant banking in the United States. If banks or other institutions could take large equity positions in the companies they lend to, it would be in their interest to stick with projects that might take four or five years to reach a payoff."

Fourth, "The U.S. can no longer afford a large pool of undereducated and even illiterate workers. . . . The U.S. simply is not spending enough for education and job training. . . . Human capital requires at least as much nurturing as currently favored financial investments."

Fifth, he argues, "Management and unions can no longer afford old-style adversarial relations. . . . [They must agree on] a new system of labor-management relations and compensation that links new technology with a fundamental restructuring of work practices . . . [and] replace the traditional division of work into narrow tasks . . . with broader jobs, rotating assignments, and considerable self management."

Finally, Jonas argues that something must be done to reverse the lead of U.S. trade rivals in the field of research and development. "R & D is the clearest case of subsidization making sense, since the innovations produced by private research generally yield benefits to the public and not just the companies footing the bill."[12]

Such an agenda is impressive and even in a free market framework would be feasible except for the fact that someone has to foot the bill. In the current antitax environment, it is not realistic to think that any political candidate could be elected on a tax-increase platform.

If taxes cannot be increased, expenditures have to be cut. Yet politically untouchable entitlements make up such a large part of the federal budget that meaningful expenditure cuts are not possible. That leaves the defense budget, the largest category in the federal budget. There is a voluminous literature that makes the case that defense expenditures could be cut without significantly reducing the national security, but so long as the United States remains committed to both its own defense and that of its allies, reductions in defense spending will not be feasible.[13] That has led some to suggest that the question of U.S. world dominance needs to be reevaluated.

The Decline of U.S. Hegemony: Who Cares?

Underlying the overall issue of the decline of U.S. dominance of the world economy is the question: Why does it matter? A 1987 survey found that 67 percent of those polled felt that the United States has "grown weaker relative to other countries," and 67 percent believed "American's industries aren't geared to keeping up with changes taking place in the world economy." Clearly Americans are concerned about the future. By 1988 several books outlining the "decline of the American empire" had made the best-seller lists. Taken together they represent a new intellectual movement, dubbed a "school of decline" by writer Peter Schmeisser.[14]

The essence of their message, perhaps most forcefully stated in Yale historian Paul Kennedy's lengthy book *The Rise and Fall of the Great Powers*, is that the United States rose to a position of economic hegemony after World War II through economic and technological achievements that allowed it to devote larger and larger proportions of its wealth to military expenditures. But as the U.S. economy has moved into a more mature stage, it has not been able to sustain its worldwide military commitments and at the same time maintain the economic growth levels requried to keep the balance of economic power tilting in its direction.[15]

The picture of this book and others like it is one of a nation overextended on all fronts, gradually slipping into second-rate status, and being forced to share power with emerging power blocs in Europe and the Pacific. This thesis has sparked lively debate in Congress and spawned several new organizations devoted to "correcting the problem." Among these is the Democratic Leadership Council of the Congress, which proposes a system of democratic capitalism—an "industrial policy" to revive the sleeping giant. Another group, Rebuild America, linked to Massachusetts governor Michael Dukakis, calls for a political consensus for a national investment strategy to improve capital formation, manufacturing technology, productivity, and job training—all within the context of the first priority: reduction of government spending. How these conflicting goals are to be reconciled with the need to reduce the federal deficit is not clear.

The issue at bottom is that the United States has to decide whether it wants to attempt to regain its position of world economic leadership while maintaining military hegemony. If it does, sacrifices have to be made. Consumption levels have to be reduced and investment has to be rechanneled toward nonmilitary sectors, such as education and research and development, that will eventually lead to increased productivity without pushing the work force into nonproductive service areas. This is not a likely scenario. The question "who cares?" has so far been answered by ever higher consumer spending, ever increasing levels of imports, and ever lower savings levels.

Why Should the United States Be Number One?

Much of the argument we have made here depends on the assumption that free trade among nations benefits everyone. Virtually all economists support the venerable theory of comparative advantage to the extent that it has become the cornerstone of international economic theory and the rationale by which all arguments for protection are summarily dismissed. But free trade has a way of bestowing advantages on the strong at the expense of the weak.[16]

Free trade benefited Great Britain during the mid-nineteenth-century period of its dominance of the world economy when it could rely on the British Empire to absorb its surpluses and supply its raw material needs. As the empire crumbled, so did the advantages of free trade, and Britain settled into a period of slower growth and lower relative standards of living. But it did not wither and fade away.

Some economists, albeit a minority, now argue that the United States has reached a similar stage in its development and that by clinging to outmoded theories of comparative advantage, it is ensuring its demise. Everyone in America bemoans the loss of U.S. dominance because it is assumed that free trade benefits America and that what is good for the United States is good for everyone else. Every policy proposal we have examined in this book presupposes that assumption. The problem is that even if every single tariff or other trade protection in the world were eliminated overnight or even if all tariffs were doubled overnight, the same problems would still be there. Japan would still be the world's largest creditor nation, the United States the largest debtor, and so on.

That fact has led some to suggest that all policy proposals designed to resolve the trade imbalance question are misdirected. Why, they ask, does everybody think the United States has to be number one? Why does it have to restructure its economy to emulate the mercantilistic policies of Japan or the low-wage-driven export strategy of the NICs? Why not, as economist David Gordon and others have asked, just tend to our own front yard? Such a "front yard" strategy, Gordon argues,

> would promote a transition away from domestic dependence on the global economy and toward cooperation with our friends and allies abroad. . . . [Why not] . . . pursue more effective domestic production of necessities—such as energy, clothing, and transportation—not indulgent succor of backward industries.[17]

In the internationally interdependent world of the 1980s, such a proposal seems like utopianism at best or a thinly disguised argument for protectionism at worst, but given the alternatives—declining living standards and loss of economic sovereignty—any proposal designed to reduce the level of U.S. import consumption makes sense if it can be accomplished without triggering retaliatory responses from the rest of the world.

Import substitution schemes are not new. In various forms they have been tried by many developing countries; Mexico's import substitution industrialization program of the 1970s is the most notable example (and a most notable failure). In many ways, the debtor status of the United States is not much different from that of most of the heavily indebted Third World countries; the major difference is that the United States has the economic power and, more important, the internal resources to implement an import substitution program if it wanted to and was ready to make the necessary sacrifices. David Gordon suggests these short-term measures:

1. Chart the sectors of the economy that are experiencing the most rapid increases in foreign imports and explore concrete domestic alternatives to those imports—for example, federal subsidies for developing conservation and renewable-energy alternatives to imported oil.

2. Negotiate trade agreements that not only aim at reductions in tariffs but also seek multilateral treaties allocating imports and exports for each participating nation. At the moment there are few such agreements, and these are largely obsolete. We need, in effect, to update GATT, first negotiated nearly forty years ago, through either a new general treaty or a set of bilateral or multilateral agreements.

3. Establish programs during the transition to a front yard economy that are aimed at cushioning the costs of adjustment for U.S. workers in affected industries, emulating (for example) the Japanese program for structurally depressed industries.

4. Adopt specific proposals such as recently debated legislation for a domestic-content requirement for automobiles. Such measures are less protectionist than quotas because they encourage production in the United States (under such legislation, foreign firms would be required to invest and produce in the United States) and expose U.S. enterprises to the best of foreign technical and managerial practice.

5. Institute plant-closing legislation designed to provide some protection to workers against the sudden flight of capital abroad by making advance notification and indemnification provisions for plant shutdowns and sudden shifts of investment abroad and by removing current tax incentives for domestic firms to invest abroad.

In the longer run, Gordon suggests, the United States may be thinking backward when it comes to restoring international competitiveness. In theory as well as practice, a key assumption has been that holding wages down and paring down the size of the work force will help competition. Fewer workers producing the same amount of goods—or more—at lower wages does, to be sure, add up to higher productivity (higher output per man-hour). But, Gordon posits, perhaps the reverse could also be true. Perhaps higher wages and better job security would increase productivity as workers were able "to identify their stake in the future of the enterprise. . . . When offered job security and promises of stable wage growth in the proper management climate . . . [workers] can actually take the initiative in spurring productivity growth."[18]

Under current and normal conditions, workers generally oppose productivity-oriented technological changes because they fear losing their jobs. Under a wage-led productivity plan, the opposite would be the case. Such a radical proposal seems unlikely to infiltrate corporate boardrooms soon, but experiments at Procter & Gamble, General Motors, General Electric, Goodyear, and many other companies have caught the attention—if not the imagination—of many corporate leaders. It is, in any case, one example of how a front yard strategy would differ from a strategy of staying on top. Workers not only produce goods but they also buy them. Higher-paid workers buy more of them.

Gordon also suggests that a different way of thinking about international trade in general would greatly reduce U.S. dependence on both imports and exports. The conventional strategy is to close the trade deficit by increasing exports while "tolerating" imports. But, he says, a tending-the-front-yard strategy "in contrast, calls for reducing both the export and the import share over the long term, while reducing the import share by a somewhat wider margin."

The increasing U.S. dependence on imported oil, which peaked in the 1970s but is growing again, is probably the clearest example of how the different strategies would work:

> Take the case of imported oil and the aftermath of the OPEC price hikes of 1973 and 1979. One response to the immediately higher costs of imports was to seek compensating increases in our exports—searching vigorously for commodities such as grain, arms, and computers for which we could find new markets abroad. Another approach could have placed a higher priority than the government did during the 1970s on reducing our dependence on imported oil—through invigorated energy-conservation programs and an emphasis on locally available and renewable sources of energy like solar and geothermal power. The former strategy might work over the short term but is likely to lose effectiveness over the longer term, because international markets and prices periodically shift. The latter strategy has clear promise for both the short and long term, because it would more or less permanently lessen our demand for a substance that is a significant component of our import bill. The former would require that we continually adjust to unexpected shocks from beyond our borders. The latter would gradually reduce our exposure to such shocks.[19]

Clearly such a strategy seems protectionist, if not pollyannish, but when put in the broader context of increasing world economic interdependence functioning on the rationale of perceived comparative advantages, one has to remember that one result of letting free markets function internationally is that wages tend to level worldwide. Therefore, while in the short run the United States may benefit from the cheap labor abroad, the end result is that U.S. wage levels will fall as others rise. To a certain extent that has been happening already, one reason that the Japanese can produce Hondas in Ohio and export them to Japan profitably. Average manufacturing wages in Japan now exceed similar wages in the United States. Ultimately, Gordon argues, it is a question of national sovereignty:

> The final major goal of international economic policy involves the question of national sovereignty. . . . While realism requires flexibility in the face of international competition, the U.S. cannot agree to abandon its standard of living or its traditional commitment to restrain exploitation of child labor, preserve the health of its workforce, protect its environment, provide retired, unemployed, or handicapped citizens with an adequate level income. . . . If we permit ourselves to become locked into the competitive "race to the bottom" we will inevitably lose control over the most basic social and political aspects of our national life.[20]

End of an Era

Whatever the theoretical subtleties, the short-term and long-term trade-offs, or the political consequences, no one can argue that we have reached the end of the era of U.S. hegemony. This was inevitable, but it was clearly speeded by the globalization of the production process, which, as Michael Moffitt and many others have pointed out, is probably the most important development of the postwar era. And it is irreversible. Moffitt makes the point clearly:

> The rise of the multinational corporation, I am increasingly convinced, represents the central macroeconomic event of the postwar world, the significance of which neither academic analysis nor policy has fully grasped. While most economists and politicians discuss world trade as if individual nations were engaged in shipping products to and from one another, the rise of multinational corporations has made these conventional concepts of world trade obsolete. Consider the facts: one-third or more of all "trade" in manufactured goods now consists of intracompany transactions by multinationals. In the last five years, foreign direct investment by U.S.-based multinationals has expanded by about 25 percent, a very respectable increase given worldwide gluts in many products. There has also been a real shift away from investment in petroleum and mining toward manufacturing, finance, and banking. Direct investment in manufacturing facilities is up nearly 30 percent since 1983. In certain industries, like machinery, it has soared more than 60 percent.

In manufacturing today, foreign jobs account for about a third of U.S. multinationals' total employment. And, according to business consultant Peter Drucker, around 20 percent of all manufacturing by U.S. multinationals is done outside of the United States. It has been estimated that multinationals import up to 40 to 50 percent of all U.S. imports, with a third of these coming in the form of intracompany transactions.[21]

During the 1960s and early 1970s, Moffitt argues, the situation was quite different. Then "the U.S. economy clearly benefited from the spread of U.S. multinationals, and the U.S. standard of living was higher as a result of their activities. [And then] . . . overseas investment by U.S.-based multinationals boosted U.S. exports of capital goods. . . . These exports . . . dwarfed U.S. capital goods imports [and] offset growing imports of televisions, radios and other consumer goods."

> But that era is over. The multinationalization of production is a result of the fact that capital is mobile and labor, by and large, is not. With the growth of worldwide sourcing, telecommunications, and money transfers, there is no pecuniary reason for U.S. firms to pay Americans to do what Mexicans or Koreans will do at a fraction of the cost. This is why "elite" U.S. working-class jobs are being sent abroad and "outsourcing" is the current rage in manufacturing. As a result, American multinationals remain highly competitive and their profits are booming, while the United States itself is becoming less and less competitive. In the 1980s, U.S. capital goods exports have collapsed while imports of both consumer and producer goods have surged, no doubt in part because U.S. firms are not importing these products from foreign lands. In other words, we once exported the capital goods used to manufacture our consumer imports; now we are also importing the capital goods to run what remains of our domestic industry.[22]

Add that to the debt explosion and the now almost total U.S. dependence on foreign capital to finance its deficits and, Moffitt argues, we have come full circle:

> Thus, we have the outlines of a true vicious circle: the world economy is dependent on growth in the U.S. economy but the U.S. domestic economy is skewed more toward consumption than production and investment, and this consumption is in turn sustained by borrowing—at home and abroad. An economy sustained by debt, especially foreign debt, is always vulnerable to an interest rate shock, whether it is administered by the Fed or by the markets. Given foreign dependence on the U.S. market, a rate shock that is great enough to send the U.S. economy into a new recession thus virtually guarantees a worldwide economic collapse with all that that implies for bankruptcies, defaults, and the widespread liquidation of debt.[23]

From a slightly different perspective, W. Michael Blumenthal, secretary of the treasury during the Carter administration and currently chairman and CEO of the Unisys Corporation, has reached similar conclusions. The problem, he argues, is that technological change has far outpaced the ability of political and economic institutions to cope with it:

> I believe there is one circumstance which overshadows all else and has set the current period apart: unprecedented, deep and continual technological change. In the 1970s and 1980s extraordinarily rapid technological change has thrust upon us new and as yet unresolved problems of governance in the national and international spheres.
>
> There appears to be a fundamental lag between the current rate of technological change and the rate of adjustment to these changes among decision-makers. Technology that evolves much more rapidly than the body politic can absorb creates strains and stresses which lead to dislocations, instabilities and paralysis of action—and sometimes perverse responses. This is what characterizes our situation today. The problem is further complicated because the private sector accepts technological change more rapidly than the government.
>
> Today's situation differs in one fundamental aspect from earlier periods of rapid technological change (e.g., during the invention of the steam engine or the telephone). The current period of revolutionary change is occurring in a much more interdependent world in which purely or largely national efforts to adapt to change have ceased to suffice. Furthermore, existing international institutions have been rendered obsolete by technological change, and the capacity for making international reforms is even less developed than that for making domestic reforms. In the absence of adequate institutions, progress on adjusting to the new technology is reduced to a slow crawl.[24]

Advances in microelectronics, Blumenthal argues, have revolutionized the production process to the point that the shift of employment to the service sector has become the issue of the decade and, as well, the challenge of the world economy:

> Service trade was not a problem . . . twenty years ago. Today, it is the issue. In an advanced country such as the United States, 75 percent of the work force is now employed in the service sector overall, and two-thirds of that number are connected in one way or another with information or with the knowledge industry itself. The estimate is that by the year 2000 only 15 percent of all employment in the United States will be devoted to the manufacture of goods.
>
> Increasingly, then, a country's comparative advantage lies in its ability to utilize effectively the new information technology, in the speed of its absorption into the productive process, and in the relative efficiency with which it is applied. Less and less it is the other factor endowments, the availability of raw materials or the cost of labor, that determines which country has the advantage and which has the lowest total cost.[25]

At bottom line the issue has become one of national sovereignty, which, Blumenthal argues, has become obsolete in all but the most philosophical sense:

> Technology is rapidly making the basic notion of national sovereignty obsolete in many areas of economic affairs—at least for some of the major nations of the world, and ultimately for most:
>
> — There is now one world capital market. How then can any major nation hope to conduct a truly effective national monetary policy all on its own?
>
> — Exchange rates quickly transmit the effects of key tax, spending and budget decisions from one major country to another. How then can there be a truly independent national fiscal policy?
>
> — Factors of production are less fixed and knowledge flows freely across borders. How then can strictly national rules and regulations remain effective if they are out of step with the rest of the world?
>
> — And if technology can rapidly override the effects, how can national import restrictions and protectionism possibly still achieve their stated aims?
>
> The conclusion is inescapable that technology has created a world no longer effectively composed of individual national economic entities. Thus, if we continue to act as if nothing has changed, our persistence in applying strictly national policies is bound to prove frustrating, and often counterproductive as well.[26]

The problem facing the world is, What role will the United States play in adjusting to this new reality? One possibility is to slide into a secondary role and forfeit leadership to Japan or Europe. This, as we have argued, is the more likely scenario. But, as Blumenthal points out, this may not be possible:

> No real progress is likely or possible without the leadership of the United States. We are no longer the dominating world economic power, but we are still the largest and most powerful nation. Ours is the world's largest single market and our currency remains at the center of international finance. We remain the political and strategic leader of the West. And we have the greatest military strength, with worldwide interests and commitments that span the globe. What happens in the United States affects world economic events profoundly. We were the principal architect of the existing framework created in the wake of the Second World War, and none of these international economic institutions can evolve without our active initiative and support.[27]

Blumenthal suggests the United States needs "to define a bold and comprehensive new philosophical underpinning for the management of domestic and international affairs . . . a new strategy," one based on five key principles.

The effort to define a new strategy must be based, first, on realism, on a willingness to think about the world as it is and not as it once was, and second, on a recognition that U.S. hegemony in economic affairs has come to an end; the triangular power bloc of the United States, Japan and the European Economic Community, and the three-currency grouping of the dollar, mark and yen has taken its place.

The third principle will be particularly difficult to put across, but strikes me as a prerequisite for intelligent progress on almost any front. We need to lead the way in redefining, for others and for ourselves, the meaning of "national interest" in broader terms than in the past. Implied here is the proposition that national interest now dictates for all a limiting of unilateral moves in economic affairs, and that for all the key actors it must encompass greater concern over the impact of major domestic measures on others. It implies acceptance of the principle of common responsibility for internationally compatible solutions to domestic needs, and for the creation of and support for the institutions necessary to coordinate these efforts on a broader scale.

The fourth principle is a corollary of the third. It involves the commitment to renounce, or at least to limit wherever possible, those measures that are particularly incompatible with the expanded definition of what the true national interest now means. Protectionist policies immediately come to mind. The unwillingness to collaborate on environmental issues, it can be argued, is another case in point.

Fifth and finally, the principle of nonexclusivity, that is, the need to take account of the broader interdependencies of economic problems affecting the many, should also be recognized and understood. Technology will tie all of us together on this earth. And more than before, broad interrelationships will have to be taken into account, whether they concern the communist bloc or the wider range of LDCs [less developed countries], and whether they deal with currency problems or the connection between market access and economic aid.[28]

Translating such challenges into concrete policies without at the same time bringing the world economy to its knees is a tall order. It is easy to point out problems. Critics of capitalism were doing that long before the trade and debt crisis and long before the stock market crash made everyone realize that the bubble had burst. Ironically what seems to underlie most of the problems and the developing crisis we have outlined in this book is not the failure of capitalism to deliver the goods but its tendency to deliver too many. The system, as Marx thought it would, produces but has not been able to distribute. Excess capacity and insufficient demand, as Keynes demonstrated, is a sure formula for recession. Mix that with record trade imbalances and an unprecedented debt explosion, and you have written the program for another Great Depression. If that is to be avoided, changes must be made. If they are not made voluntarily, they will be imposed at a cost much higher than we can imagine.

As the thoughtful reader will no doubt point out, there are many contradictions in the varied lines of argument we have examined here. On the one hand, it seems logical, if not sagacious, to argue that the current imbalance problems could and should be solved if the United States would—and could—put its own house in order. Making the U.S. economy more productive and competitive in order to reverse the current disturbing trade balance trends might restore the world economy to levels it enjoyed during the 1960s and 1970s, when it was dominated by U.S. economic power and fed by increasing levels of consumption amid rising incomes.

But to argue for that highly unlikely scenario while at the same time stressing the need for increased international coordination between the United States and the rapidly emerging economic power blocs does not fit well with the specter of reality that is haunting the world economy today. International policy coordination requires externally imposed discipline, and, more important, it requires that someone give up something. Until someone is willing to do that, the trend lines, which have already crossed into an abyss of imbalance, will continue to diverge. At some point they will go off the charts. When that happens it will be time to talk.

Meanwhile, as a beginning, the time has come for the major players to sit down at the same table and begin to consider ways in which the international financial system can be restructured to reflect the realities of the modern world. Some would call it a new Bretton Woods conference. We would call it a poker game in which the United States is no longer the dealer and the banker. Whatever it is called, it will be a very high stakes game.

Notes

Chapter 1

1. Jacques de Larosiere, address to the joint meetings of the IMF and World Bank, Washington, D.C., September 1986.
2. *New York Times*, June 11, 1987, p. 16A.
3. Ibid., November 6, 1987.

Chapter 2

1. Alfred Malabre, *Beyond Our Means* (New York: Random House, 1987).
2. Ibid., p. 75.
3. The rest is portfolio investment—corporate stocks and bonds and governmental securities.
4. Ernest Conine, *Los Angeles Times*, June 15, 1988.
5. That is, the amount they are owed exceeds the total value of their shareholders' equity—the book value of their stock outstanding.
6. Donald Regan, testimony before U.S. Congress, House Banking, Finance and Urban Affairs Committee, December 21, 1982.

Chapter 3

1. Morris Miller, *Coping Is Not Enough: The International Debt Crisis and the Roles of the World Bank and the IMF* (Homewood, Ill.: Irwin, 1987), pp. 169–170.
2. Henry Kissinger, "The Future of the Global Economy," *Washington Post*, November 22, 1984; Miller, *Coping*, p. 143.
3. Miller, *Coping*, p. 146.
4. Irving S. Friedman, *Toward World Prosperity* (Lexington, Mass.: Lexington Books, 1986), pp. 291–293.
5. Martin Feldstein, "The End of Policy Coordination," *New York Times*, November 9, 1987.

6. Robert Kuttner, "The Theory Gap," *New York Times*, January 17, 1988.

7. Ibid.

8. Ibid.

9. Ibid.

10. Deborah Allen Oliver, "Few Industries Benefit from the Weaker Dollar," *Wall Street Journal*, January 30, 1987.

11. Michael Hudson, "A Cheap Dollar Won't Cure the Deficit," *New York Times*, January 24, 1988.

12. Paul Farba, "Hidden Dangers of Currency Cooperation," *Wall Street Journal*, November 23, 1987.

13. Ronald I. McKinnon, "A Model for Currency Cooperation," *Wall Street Journal*, September 21, 1987; McKinnon, "When Capital Flowed and Exchange Rates Held," *Wall Street Journal*, March 28, 1988; McKinnon, "Monetary and Exchange Rate Policies for International Financial Stability: A Proposal, "*Journal of Economic Perspectives* 2, no. 1 (Winter 1988): 83–103; McKinnon, *An International Standard for Monetary Stabilization* (Washington, D.C.: Institute for International Economics, 1984). See also Rudiger Dornbusch, "Doubts about the McKinnon Standard," and John Williamson, "Comment on McKinnon's Monetary Rule," *Journal of Economic Perspectives* 2, no. 1 (Winter 1988): 105–112 and 113–119, respectively.

14. John Williamson and Marcus H. Miller, *Targets and Indicators: A Blueprint for the International Coordination of Economic Policy* (Washington, D.C.: Institute for International Economics, September 1987).

15. Edward Balladur, "Rebuilding an International Monetary System," *Wall Street Journal*, February 23, 1988.

16. "Banks Step Up Third World Debt Disposal," *Wall Street Journal*, July 26, 1988.

17. Miller, *Coping*, p. 176.

18. John Loxley, *Debt and Disorder: External Financing for Development* (Boulder, Colo.: Westview Press, 1986), pp. 44–50.

19. Stanley Fischer, "Sharing the Burden of the International Debt Crisis," *American Economic Review* 77, no. 2 (May 1985): 165–170.

20. Jeffrey D. Sachs, "It's the Right Time to Offer Real Relief," *New York Times*, August 9, 1987.

21. William R. Cline, *Mobilizing Bank Lending to Debtor Countries* (Washington, D.C.: Institute for International Economics, June 1987), pp. 80–92.

22. Clyde Farnsworth, "IMF Studying Plan to Ease Debt Burden," *New York Times*, March 8, 1988.

23. World Bank, *World Development Report* (Washington, D.C.: World Bank, 1987), chap. 2; International Monetary Fund, *World Economic Outlook* (Washington, D.C.: IMF, April 1988).

24. Peter Truell and Matt Moffitt, "Meager Debt-Swap Results Force Mexico, Other Countries to Explore Alternatives," *Wall Street Journal*, March 7, 1988; James D. Robinson III, "It's Time to Plan a Third-World Revival," *New York Times,* August 28, 1988.

25. Harry Magdoff and Paul Sweezy, "International Cooperation—A Way Out?" *Monthly Review* (November 1987): 18–19.

Chapter 4

1. "Wake Up, America," *Business Week*, November 16, 1987.
2. Alfred Malabre, *Beyond Our Means* (New York: Basic Books, 1987).
3. "The 1980's Are Over, Greed Goes out of Style," *Newsweek*, January 4, 1988.
4. Peter Peterson, "The Morning After," *Atlantic Monthly* (October 1987): 60.
5. Ibid.
6. Ibid., p. 64.
7. Ibid., p. 49.
8. Ibid., p. 50.
9. Ibid., p. 52.
10. Barry Bluestone and Bennett Harrison, "The Grim Truth about the Job Miracle," *New York Times*, February 1, 1987.
11. E. Gerald Corrigan, "A Balanced Approach to the LDC Debt Problem," *Quarterly Review* (Federal Reserve Bank of New York) (Spring 1988): 1–6.
12. Michael Moffitt, "Economic Decline, Reagan Style: Dollar, Debt, and Deflation," *World Policy* 2, no. 3 (Summer 1985): 580.

Chapter 5

1. Paul Kennedy, *The Rise and Fall of the Great Powers* (New York: Random House, 1988); Louis Uchitelle, "When the World Lacks a Leader," *New York Times*, January 31, 1988.
2. Uchitelle, "When the World," p. F6.
3. Michele Fratianni, "Europe's Non-Model for Stable World Money," *Wall Street Journal*, April 4, 1988.
4. Edouard Balladur, "Rebuilding an International Monetary System," *Wall Street Journal*, February 23, 1988.

Chapter 6

1. Alan Sinai, "The Crash of 1987 and the Economy of 1988," *Challenge* (January–February, 1988): 11–21. See also Sinai, "The Question Is Not If, But When?" *New York Times*, April 3, 1988.
2. Sinai, "Crash," pp. 12–13.
3. Ibid., p. 16.
4. Peter Peterson, "After an Economic Heart Attack," *Newsweek*, November 2, 1987; also see Peterson, "No Pain, No Gain: How America Can Grow Again," *Business Week*, April 20, 1988.
5. Peterson, "After an Economic Heart Attack," p. 53.
6. Ibid.
7. I.M. Destler, *American Trade Politics: System under Stress* (Washington, D.C.: Institute for International Economics, 1986), p. 184.

8. Robert Reich, *The Next American Frontier* (New York: Times Books, 1983), p. 238.

9. Martin K. Starr, ed., *Global Competitiveness: Getting the U.S. Back on Track* (New York: Norton, 1988); Michael J. Piore and Charles F. Sabel, *The Second Industrial Divide: Possibilities for Prosperity* (New York: Basic Books, 1984).

10. Robert Reich, *Tales of a New America* (New York: Times Books, 1987); and Reich, "Behold! We Do Have an Industrial Policy," *New York Times*, May 22, 1988.

11. Destler, *American Trade Politics*, p. 196.

12. Norman Jonas, "A Strategy for Revitalizing Industry," *Business Week*, March 3, 1988, p. 85.

13. Thomas Riddell, "Military Buildup, Economic Decline," *Dollars and Sense* (September 1987): 6–9; Rich West, "Military Mania," *Sane World* (Summer 1987): 10–13.

14. Peter Schmeisser, "Is America in Decline?" *New York Times Magazine*, April 17, 1988, p. 24.

15. Paul Kennedy, *The Rise and Fall of the Great Powers* (New York: Random House, 1987).

16. John C. Pool and Stephen C. Stamos, Jr., *The ABC's of International Finance* (Lexington, Mass.: Lexington Books, 1987), pp. 17–24.

17. David Gordon, "Do We Need to Be No. 1?" *Atlantic Monthly* (April 1986): 103. See also Samuel Bowles, David Gordon, and Thomas Weisskopf, *Beyond the Wasteland* (New York: Basic Books, 1983).

18. Gordon, "Do We Need to Be No. 1?", p. 105

19. Ibid.

20. Ibid., p. 106.

21. Michael Moffitt, "Shocks, Deadlocks, and Scorched Earth: Reaganomics and the Decline of U.S. Hegemony," *World Policy* (Spring 1987): 557.

22. Ibid., p. 559.

23. Ibid., p. 560.

24. W. Michael Blumenthal, "The World Economy and Technological Change," *Foreign Affairs* (Spring 1988): 531.

25. Ibid., p. 543.

26. Ibid., p. 545.

27. Ibid., p. 546.

28. Ibid., p. 547.

Bibliography

Amuzegar, Jahangir. "Dealing with Debt." *Foreign Policy*, no. 68 (Fall 1987).

Bergsten, C. Fred, and William R. Cline. *The United States–Japan Economic Problem.* Washington, D.C.: Institute for International Economics, October 1985.

Block, Fred. *The Origins of International Economic Disorder.* Berkeley: University of California Press, 1977.

Bowles, Samuel, David Gordon, and Thomas Weisskopf. *Beyond the Wasteland.* Garden City, N.Y.: Anchor/Doubleday, 1982.

Cline, William R., *International Debt and the Stability of the World Economy.* Washington, D.C.: Institute for International Economics, 1983.

———. *Mobilizing Bank Lending to Debtor Countries.* Washington, D.C.: Institute for International Economics, 1987.

Destler, I.M. *American Trade Politics: System under Stress.* Washington, D.C.: Institute for International Economics, 1986.

Epstein, Gerald. "The Triple Debt Crisis." *World Policy* 2, no. 4 (Fall 1985).

Friedman, Irving S. *Toward World Prosperity* Lexington, Mass.: Lexington Books, 1986.

Gordon, David. "Do We Need to Be No. 1?" *Atlantic Monthly* (April 1986).

Griffin, Keith. *Alternative Strategies for Economic Development* New York: St. Martin's Press, 1988.

Griffith-Jones, Stephanie, ed. *Managing World Debt.* New York: St. Martin's, 1988.

Griffith-Jones, Stephanie, and Osvaldo Sunkel. *Debt and Development in Latin America: The End of an Illusion.* New York: Oxford University Press, 1986.

Gray, H. Peter. *International Economic Problems and Policies.* New York: St. Martin's, Press, 1987.

"Human Capital: The Decline of America's Work Force." *Business Week*, September 19, 1988.

Inter-American Development Bank. *Economic and Social Progress Report.* Washington, D.C.: IADB, 1987.

International Monetary Fund. *World Economic Outlook.* Washington, D.C.: IMF, April 1988.

Kaletsky, Anatole. *The Costs of Default,* New York: Priority Press, 1985.

Kennedy, Paul. *The Rise and Fall of the Great Powers.* New York: Random House, 1988.

Kolko, Joyce. *Restructuring the World Economy.* New York: Pantheon, 1988.

Krugman, Paul R., ed. *Strategic Trade Policy and the New International Economics.* Cambridge: MIT Press, 1987.

Kuczynski, Pedro-Pablo. *Latin American Debt.* Baltimore: Johns Hopkins University Press, 1988.

Lawrence, Robert Z., *Can America Compete?* Washington, D.C.: Brookings Institution, 1984.

Lessard, Donald R., and John Williamson. *Financial Intermediation beyond the Debt Crisis.* Washington, D.C.: Institute for International Economics, 1985.

———. *Capital Flight and Third World Debt.* Washington, D.C.: Institute for International Economics, 1987.

Lever, Harold, and Christopher Huhne. *Debt and Danger: The World Financial Crisis.* New York: Atlantic Monthly Press, 1985.

Loxley, John. *Debt and Disorder: External Financing for Development.* Boulder, Colo.: Westview Press, 1986.

McKinnon, Ronald I. *An International Standard for Monetary Stabilization.* Washington, D.C.: Institute for International Economics, 1984.

Makin, John H. *The Global Debt Crisis: America's Growing Involvement.* New York: Basic Books, 1984.

Malabre, Alfred. *Beyond Our Means.* New York: Random House, 1987.

Marris, Stephen. *Deficits and the Dollar: The World Economy at Risk.* Washington, D.C.: Institute for International Economics, 1988.

Miller, Morris. *Coping Is Not Enough: The International Debt Crisis and the Roles of the World Bank and the International Monetary Fund.* Homewood, Ill.: Irwin, 1986.

Peterson, Peter. "The Morning After." *Atlantic Monthly* (October 1987).

Piore, Michael J., and Charles F. Sabel. *The Second Industrial Divide.* New York: Basic Books, 1984.

Pirog, Robert, and Stephen C. Stamos. *Energy Economics: Theory and Policy.* Englewood Cliffs, N.J.: Prentice-Hall, 1987.

Pool, John Charles, and Stephen C. Stamos. *The ABC's of International Finance.* Lexington, Mass.: Lexington Books, 1987.

Pool, John Charles, and Ross M. LaRoe. *Default.* New York: St. Martin's Press, 1987.

———. *The Instant Economist.* Reading, Mass.: Addison-Wesley, 1985.

Reich, Robert B. *The Next American Frontier.* New York: Times Books, 1983.

———. *Tales of a New America.* New York: Times Books, 1987.

Resolving the Global Economic Crisis: After Wall Street. A Statement by Thirty-three Economists from Thirteen Countries. Special Report 6. Washington, D.C.: Institutes for International Economics, December 1987.

Riddell, Thomas, Jean Shackelford, and Stephen C. Stamos. *Economics: A Tool for Understanding Society.* 3d ed. Reading, Mass.: Addison-Wesley, 1987.

Starr, Martin K., ed. *Global Competitiveness: Getting the U.S. Back on Track.* New York: Norton, 1988.

Wachtel, Howard. *The Money Mandarins: The Making of a Supranational Economic Order.* New York: Pantheon, 1986.

Weidenbaum, Murray. *Rendezvous with Reality: The American Economy after Reagan.* New York: Basic Books, 1988.

Williamson, John. *The Exchange Rate System*. Washington, D.C.: Institute for International Economics, 1983.

Williamson, John, and Marcus H. Miller. *Targets and Indicators: A Blueprint for the International Coordination of Economic Policy*. Washington, D.C.: Institute for International Economics, 1987.

World Bank. *World Debt Tables: External Debt of Developing Countries*. vol. 1: *Analysis and Summary Tables*. Washington, D.C.: World Bank, 1988.

Index

140 • *International Economic Policy*

Exports/imports: *(Continued)*
programs, 129; increases in, 1980–86,
105; and Third World economy,
40–41; U.S., export increases, 30, 93

Federal budget, components of, 83, 84
Federal debt, 24–36; barnyard perspective,
24; components of, 25, 29–30; compounding and, 26–28; foreign investment and, 36; interest payments and,
26; net external assets, 33; ownership
of, 26; as percentage of GNP, 27;
public finance perspective, 25; taxes
and, 28, 76; U.S. compared to Third
World, 36; U.S. as debtor nation,
30–32, 36, 51–52, 91–92. *See also*
U.S. economy, Policy needs
Federal deficit, 114, 117; Reagan administration, 28
Feldstein, Martin, 58
Fischer, Stanley, 67
Foreign investment: cash outflow problem,
35; future scenarios, 35; government
securities owned, 32–33; interest rates
and, 31, 35, 97; real estate, 35, 102;
U.S. corporation ownership, 30–34,
102. *See also* Japan
Fratianni, Michele, 111
Friedman, Irving, 55
Fundamental equilibrium exchange rate, 62

General Agreement on Tariffs and Trade, 21
Glass-Steagall Act, 120
Global economy, excess capacity in, 59–60
Gold: fall in reserves, 7–8; role in interna-
tional finance, 2–3; standard, re-
quirements for, 2–3
Gordon, David, 122–125
Gramm-Rudman deficit reduction law, 79
Great Depression, 30, 77, 129
Greenspan Commission, 89
Gross national product (GNP), comparative
view, 100, 106

Hegemony, 106–107; decline of U.S., 121,
122, 125–129; requirements for, 107;
results of, 106–107
Hospital Insurance program, 87, 89
Hudson, Michael, 60

Imports: import substitution programs,
129. *See also* Exports/imports
Industrial policy, and competitiveness, 118
Inflation: Keynesian approach, 76; U.S.,
1970–80s, 51; worldwide, 55
Interest payments: compounding, 26–28;
federal debt and, 26

Interest rates: and foreign investment, 31,
35; low, effects of, 59, 97; recession
and, 82
International economy: future scenarios,
107–108, 110; hegemony, 106–107;
trading blocks, 108, 110
International financial system: Bretton
Woods Conference, 3–4; dollar glut,
development of, 4–6; Eurodollar market,
6–7; exchange payments standardization
proposals, 49, 57; fall in gold reserves,
7–8; role of gold, 2–3; International
Monetary Fund, 4, 12–13; Mexican
crisis, 15–16; oil embargo, 8–12;
Petrodollar recycling, 8–9; Plaza Agreement, 16–18; strong dollar syndrome,
13–14, 17; Venice summit, 18–22
International Monetary Fund, 4, 12–13;
conservation of, 53; exchange rate
monitoring, 50

Japan: assets in U.S., 34, 101, 103; as
creditor nation, 31, 34, 46, 52; culture,
effects of, 99–100; current account
balance, 100, 102; economic growth,
explanation of, 99–100; economic
strategy, mercantilism, 104; future
view, 102; investments in U.S., 33–35,
100, 102–104; productivity rate, 95;
savings, 100; and U.S. economic future,
102, 104; world leadership shared with
U.S., 107–108
J-curve theory, 17, 58
Jonas, Norman, 119

Kenen, Peter, 68
Kennedy, Paul, 107, 121
Keynesian economics, 76
Keynes, John Maynard, 3
Kissinger, Henry, 53
Krugman, Paul, 58
Kuttner, Robert, 58, 59

Labor: and industry, 119
Laffer curve, 75
Louvre Accord, 60
Loxley, John, 66

McKinnon, Robert, 61
Macroeconomic policy, 116–117; choosing
right policies, 116–117
Manufacturing sector: competitiveness and,
95–96; job decline, 96
Mercantilism, 2; Japan, 104
Mexican crisis, 15–16, 96; foreign debt,
1970–88, 71; zero coupon bonds experiment, 70, 72

About the Authors

John Charles Pool received his B.A. and M.B.A. from the University of Missouri and the Ph.D. in economics from the University of Colorado. He is coauthor of *Economia: Enfoque America Latina* (1982), *The Instant Economist* (1985), *The ABCs of International Finance* (Lexington Books, 1987), *Default!* (1987), and author of *Studying and Thinking about Economics and Society* (1986), and has published numerous articles on various topics in economics. He also writes (with Ross M. LaRoe) a syndicated newspaper column, "The Instant Economist," which treats current issues in economics.

Dr. Pool has taught at Bucknell University and the Universities of Iowa and Missouri. For two years he was a Fulbright Professor in Mexico and currently is an adjunct professor of Economics at St. John Fisher College. He is head of Charles Pool & Associates in Rochester, New York, a firm which specializes in research and writing in the field of managerial and international economics.

Stephen C. Stamos, Jr., received his B.A. from San Diego State University, an M.S. in economics from Wright State University, and the Ph.D. in political economy from the Union Graduate School. He is coauthor of *Economics: A Tool for Understanding Society* (Third Ed. 1986) and *Energy Economics: Theory and Policy* (1986), and *The ABCs of International Finance* (Lexington Books, 1987), and has published widely in professional journals on the topics of energy and international economics.

Dr. Stamos is professor of economics at Bucknell University. He has also been a visiting professor at Evergreen State College and at the University of Massachusetts–Amherst, and has been a visiting fellow at the Center for U.S.–Mexico Studies, The University of California–San Diego.

Pool and Stamos have collaborated on several studies of Latin American economic issues and problems, including a major study of the role of tourism in the Mexican economy and another on Mexican external debt. They have both lived and taught in Mexico.

Copyright Acknowledgments